Mortar
& Pestle

Mortar & Pestle

Classic Indonesian Recipes for the Modern Kitchen

• Patricia Tanumihardja and Juliana Evari Suparman •

weldon**owen**

Contents

Chapter 3

One-Dish Meals / Makanan Sederhana

Chapter 4

Let's Grill! / Ayo Panggang!

An Introduction

How I Learned to Cook

"Keruk, keruk, keruk . . ." The sound of stone grinding against stone is both familiar and comforting to me. I spent many afternoons by my mum's side as she ground various spice pastes called bumbu bumbu—the foundation of many Indonesian dishes—with her trusty mortar and pestle.

When I was growing up in Singapore, our house had two kitchens. The indoor kitchen, with its gleaming countertops and sparkling clean electric stove, was obviously just for show. However, you wouldn't fail to notice the well-worn tile by the back door. This was where the magic happened.

On most days, my mum, Julia, could be found squatting on a wooden stool, pumping her arm up and down as she turned a mélange of herbs and spices into bumbu bumbu. Some days, the roughly hewn basalt mortar would hold fresh turmeric or candlenuts and on other days, coriander seeds and chilies. But shallots and garlic were always a must. Often, you'd find me next to her, my brow furrowed in concentration, pounding carrot peels or discarded shards of ginger as I played masak masak (cook cook).

The real action took place outside by the grease-splattered stove with roaring burners. Here, Julia would deep-fry Ayam Goreng Manis (Sweet Fried Chicken, page 58) and sauté her incredibly pungent Julia's Sambal Terasi (page 169). She would spear chunks of terasi (shrimp paste) with a satay stick and toast it over an open flame flickering from the gas stove. The shrimp paste would then go into a hot wok, and the pungent fumes would swirl and eddy

The extended Tanumihardja family on a beautiful Seattle summer day, June 2017.

in the air, dispersing everywhere. It was then that I'd made my speedy exit, done with my cooking lesson for the day.

This was how I learned to cook, by observing and mimicking Julia in the kitchen. These moments with her were priceless. I observed every sizzle, crackle, and pop. I smelled aromas sharp and mellow. All my senses were engaged and at every step, there was a lesson to be learned.

My Family Story Told Across Three Countries

Indonesia

Julia was born in Bekasi, on the island of Java, and my dad, Rudy, several hours away in Cirebon. Eventually, they met and married in the capital, Jakarta, in 1971. They spent their first year as a newly married couple in Balikpapan, East Kalimantan (Borneo), where Rudy sold heavy equipment (think tractors and cranes). At that time, Balikpapan was very remote. With nothing much to do, Julia dove head-on into the nesting duties of a newlywed wife. She cooked meals not only for my dad but also for his employees, and Julia had to learn fast. And so she did, absorbing skills and information from cookbooks and the local ibu ibu (ladies) who helped her in the kitchen.

Once a week, Julia rushed to the docks. She wanted to be among the first to greet the boat that arrived in the early morning from nearby Surabaya with meat, chicken, and fresh vegetables. In the evening, fishermen knocked on my parents' door to offer their daily catch. "Beli dong, bu" (Please buy my fish, ma'am), they'd plead. This was probably when and where Julia developed her sharp bargaining skills.

In 1972, Rudy was transferred to Jakarta—where my brother, Marcellino (Mars), was born. That same year, the family of three moved to Singapore. Not long after, Julia was expecting me. Although I was "made in Singapore," I was born in Jakarta. Maureen (Mo), my younger sister by six years, was born in Singapore.

Soon after the wedding, Rudy and Julia moved from Jakarta to Balikpapan, Kalimantan (the Indonesian part of Borneo), where they established their first home as a married couple, c. 1973.

Singapore

Even though we didn't live in our homeland, Julia endeavored to keep us connected to our Indonesian roots. Up until preschool, Mars and I only spoke Indonesian. By the time Maureen was born, we all spoke English at home.

Julia cooked myriad Indonesian and Indonesian-Chinese dishes. We always had krupuk, sambal, and kecap manis at meals. And we celebrated Christmas with Nasi Kuning (Yellow Celebration Rice, page 178) and Ayam Goreng Kuning (Tumeric Fried Chicken, page 51) on the table right next to the baked ham.

Rudy and Julia were some of the first Indonesian expats in Singapore. They formed KKIS (Keluarga Katolik Indonesia, Singapura, or Catholic Families, Singapore) and were very active in the growing Indonesian community.

Since an Indonesian gathering isn't complete without food, Julia always obliged with a lavish spread, starting her prep at least a week before the event.

Friends flocked to our house for the huge parties Rudy and Julia hosted. Word spread that Julia was an excellent and generous cook. Our dining table overflowed with food—Gado Gado (page 123), Mi Goreng (Fried Noodles, page 110), Sate Ayam (Chicken Satay, page 129), and more. Since Julia believed that too much food was better than not enough food, our guests would always go home with doggie bags.

To keep up with our Indonesian language skills and stay in touch with family, we flew to Jakarta every year, often making side trips to Bandung, central Java, and Bali.

Life was pretty much the same until Mars left to go to college in Seattle, Washington, and I followed the next year.

Mars, Mo, and Pat on a trip to Penang, Malaysia, c. 1982.

United States

In his senior year in college, Mars was awarded an immigrant visa through the Diversity Visa Program (also known as the green card lottery). This was the first step in bringing my parents over to the United States. In 2002 , Julia and Rudy left their home of thirty years and migrated to Seattle to be close to their children and grandchildren.

The transition was not always smooth, but Julia soon found a niche. Trained to cook in large quantities right from the start, she found her calling in catering for homesick Indonesian students who missed the food of their homeland.

Then, in 2008, Julia and my sister-in-law, Yusi Sasmitra, opened Julia's Indonesian Kitchen in Seattle's Roosevelt neighborhood. Hence, Julia introduced Indonesian home cooking to the Seattle community. The restaurant was named one of the Northwest's best restaurants in its first year, and it was hugely popular. On weekends, lines snaked out the door and along the street.

Even though the restaurant was successful, Julia and Yusi decided to sell it a few years later. Much to the disappointment of many patrons, the restaurant transferred ownership in 2011.

Why I Wrote This Book

Despite its sumptuousness, Indonesian cuisine isn't as well known as its Southeast Asian counterparts such as Thai or Filipino.

It is essentially a home-cooked cuisine, every household producing a unique version of any one dish. Since recipes were not written down and followed, the oral tradition of passing them down from one generation to the next played an important role. It was only after the post-independence rise in literacy that the first Indonesian cookbook was published. *Mustikarasa* (*The Crown of Taste*), published by the Department of Agriculture in 1967, contains two thousand recipes sent in by women's organizations from across the country.

Unfortunately, even the younger generation of Indonesians today has trouble recreating family recipes, having left the culinary conjuring to mothers, grandmothers, or the domestic help.

I wanted to remedy this situation.

Julia has a long tradition of cooking for others— her family, her friends, and homesick expats and students. Over the decades, many people have asked for her recipes or, better yet, asked her to cook for them over and over again.

Julia and daughter-in-law Yusi Sasmitra owned an Indonesian restaurant in Seattle's Roosevelt neighborhood.

I am truly blessed that Julia has written down her most-cooked recipes for me to have as guidance. This cookbook is an extension of Julia's lifetime vocation, a way to share our family's recipes with the world.

Every single recipe in this cookbook has provenance. Most of them are dishes that Julia cooked for us when we were growing up. A few have been incorporated into my culinary repertoire over the years. Since my family is from Java, the recipes are mostly Javanese and Sundanese, sometimes with a Singaporean or American twist!

About Indonesia and Its Cuisine

Indonesia consists of five main islands and some thirty smaller archipelagoes, totaling about 18,110 islands. It is the largest archipelago in the world to form a single state and spans 3.8 million square miles. The country's strategic location along major sea routes has conditioned its cultural, economic, social, and political patterns over the centuries.

There are 1,340 recognized ethnic groups in Indonesia, the largest being the Javanese who make up about 40 percent of the total population.

Trade and seafaring have always been necessary because of the uneven distribution of natural resources across the islands. The Moluccas Spice Islands (now Maluku) were always a big draw. Even before European explorers set off on voyages of discovery during the sixteenth and seventeenth centuries, merchants and traders from China, India, the Middle East, and neighboring Siam and Malacca flocked to the archipelago. As a result, each region has its own distinct cuisine shaped by multiple influences.

Sumatran cuisine often has Middle Eastern and Indian influences, featuring curried meat and vegetables, while Javanese cuisine is mostly indigenous with a hint of Chinese influence. The cuisines of Eastern Indonesia are similar to that of Polynesia and Melanesia. In addition, the Dutch influence resulted in a fascinating amalgam of foods: casseroles and snacks like roti sosis (sausage rolls) and a robust tradition of baking cakes and cookies.

Indonesian food is often described as savory, hot, and spicy, with the basic tastes of sweet, salty, sour, and bitter present in most dishes. Overall, the cuisine is rich and complex, thanks to the abundance of aromatic herbs and native spices that are blended together.

The Dutch Influence on Indonesian Cuisine

Before becoming the Republic of Indonesia, the Dutch East Indies was a Dutch colony for over three hundred years. The Dutch left many legacies, and my family was a direct beneficiary.

My dad, Rudy, was born in 1939, the year World War II started in Europe. His father, my opa, was a Dutch civil servant, and the family spoke Dutch at home. Rudy went to Dutch schools and considered Dutch his first language. When I talk to him about this period in his life, he feels no animosity for the colonists. Opa had a lengthy tenure as a well-regarded postal official, and his wife and nine children were well taken care of, especially after the atrocities of the Japanese occupation in the Dutch East Indies. (Opa was charged with being a spy and imprisoned for the duration of the Japanese occupation, 1942–1945.)

Not surprisingly, some of the food we eat also has a distinct Dutch influence. This cultural and culinary union is fascinating, but I wouldn't call it fusion; it's more of an evolution as techniques, flavors, and ingredients collided and combined over centuries.

Since Indonesia has had so many external influences over its long history, it's not always possible to trace a dish's exact provenance. "Indonesia takes all culinary influences for granted and [no origin is mentioned]," says Indonesian culinary expert William Wongso. "[It's all considered] regional cooking."

However, I am confident that the Dutch are the reason why Indonesia has such a rich baking heritage. Tarts, kue basah (cakes), and kue kering (cookies) are very much a part of our culinary culture.

You may have heard of rijsttafel? It probably emerged as the European interpretation of the local tradition of indigenous communal eating. While the dishes served were very much Indonesian, rijsttafel was definitely an obnoxious way for the colonists to enjoy an extravagant variety of foods.

Dutch dignitaries served rijsttafel to impress guests with the exoticism and rich culture of their colony. When they threw dinner parties, as many as 150 items were served during a single meal, says Wongso. Most of the dishes were Javanese, but they were served Dutch-style, each on a separate plate, by white-suited, barefoot waiters.

Above all, the rijsttafel "was a statement of Dutch authority, underlined by the adoption of indigenous foods [and] adaptation of selected local dishes," says Fadly Rahman, author of *Rijsttafel: Budaya Kuliner di Indonesia masa Kolonial* (Rijsttafel: Culinary Culture in Indonesia During Colonial Times).

When Indonesia declared independence in 1945, rijsttafel, along with many other Dutch colonial customs, were rejected. Since then, they either disappeared or were integrated seamlessly into Indonesian culture.

Today, dishes like Kroket Kentang (page 27), Pastel Panggang (page 114), and the infamous layered cake, kue lapis legit, are still popular in Indonesia but are not regarded as Dutch, not even as a shared heritage, but as solely Indonesian. In fact, they are considered "memorabilia," part of Indonesia's past, explains Wongso. "We never mention these dishes are influenced by the Dutch except when asked."

Opa Rudy and Oma Julia have five grandsons (L to R): Iman, Isaac, Nathaniel (in lap), and Gabriel. Xander, the youngest, wasn't born yet.

Julia and Pat's Guide to Cooking Indonesian Food

Indonesian cuisine is a home-cooked cuisine. And the first rule of home cooking is that there aren't any hard and fast rules to follow. Consider the recipes and tips in this book as guidelines to help you discover your very own culinary journey.

Like many Indonesians, Julia cooks instinctually. Remember, for centuries there were no recipes written down and followed. Before the first Indonesian cookbook was published in the 1960s, recipes were passed down by word of mouth, from one generation to the next. Quantities for spice pastes, sambals, and complete dishes were committed to memory. Ingredients were selected and measured by sight, smell, feel, and especially taste.

Trust Your Palate and Taste as You Go

I have interpreted Julia's recipes using American measurements as best I could. But I don't want you to be bound by precision. The recipes are merely guidelines for you to discover how a dish is roughly supposed to taste. Your taste buds have the final say.

When developing the recipes in this book, I have tried to strike a middle ground. However, you should know that Julia, who absolutely has a Javanese sweet tooth, is very liberal with both sugar and kecap manis. If a recipe calls for 3 tablespoons of kecap manis, you may want to add less (or more). Also know that I am a total wuss when it comes to spice. If only two bird's eye chilies sounds lame to you, add as many as you like! In other words, don't take the quantities as absolute measures. However, I recommend starting with less. You can always add more, but it is harder to take away.

No two people cook the same dish in exactly the same way, and that includes Julia and me. The only way to make a dish taste good is to taste as you go. If seasonings are lacking, keep adding until you're happy.

Cook with Your Senses

Use all your senses when you're cooking. Smell spice pastes and taste coconut milk before you add them to a dish. Familiarize yourself with visual clues—for example, the shimmer of hot oil when it is ready. Learn to listen to the sizzle of garlic or the gurgle of curry to gauge when to move on to the next step. Most importantly, taste dishes to learn what you like and don't like. Experiment and discover how just a pinch of salt or sugar can take a dish from blah to bellissima!

By paying close attention to what you're doing and why, you'll understand how a dish comes together as well as fine-tune your palate.

Substitutions Are Okay

I'm the first to admit that Indonesian recipes often require a lot of ingredients. I'm also the first to say that it's okay to omit hard-to-find ones (say, salam leaves). In some recipes, it's fine to substitute with more of another herb. Honestly, any popular herbs—lemongrass, galangal, makrut lime leaves—combined with sweet, salty, bitter, and sour tastes will give your dish a distinct Indonesian flavor. Even if you have to replace galangal with ginger, go ahead!

Time Constraints

There's no denying that some recipes are time consuming and labor intensive. But these steps and ingredients are necessary to create the complex, layer-upon-layer flavors of our dishes. However, the recipe steps almost always can be divided up over a few days. All it takes is some planning and maybe a few extra hands to help. The resulting dish will be well worth the effort. I've offered a few shortcuts to save time and effort but only when it doesn't sacrifice too much in the result.

Traditional versus Modern Methods

The Indonesian way of prepping and cooking may not always make sense in a Western context. However, these methods have been passed down through the generations, and they are the way they are. Some examples include the multiple-step process Julia takes to cook glutinous rice for Lemper Ayam (page 33) and, of course, grinding with a mortar and pestle instead of using a food processor.

I know that Julia suns her shallots before deep-frying them because it's what her mother did. Do I? Nope. So you see, even I take shortcuts. My dishes don't always turn out exactly like Julia's do, but in the end, it's my choice, and yours, too.

Try, Try, and Try Again

I didn't try cooking Indonesian food on my own until I went away to college. Even though I was able to get some recipes from Julia over the phone, I still had to rely on my taste memory to finetune the dishes I loved as a child. They didn't always taste the way I remembered, but it was a start. After twenty years and many trials and errors, I can finally say that I can cook my favorite dishes *almost* as good as Julia can.

Similarly, you might not get some of the recipes right on the first try—or even on the second and third tries. But please don't give up. Keep trying. Keep tweaking. Practice makes progress, and even if you never get to perfect, that's okay! You're learning new ingredients, new flavors, and new techniques.

In the end, as long as you have the essential ingredients in the correct proportions, you can do whatever you want to make the dish taste good for your family and your guests.

Indonesians love to ngemil, or snack! In fact, we snack all throughout the day and even at mealtimes! Let me explain. There's a type of snack, or cemilan, called krupuk (page 193) that's usually eaten with a meal to whet the appetite. Kripik, krupuk's cousin, are smaller sweet or savory crisps made by thinly slicing tubers, fruit, or vegetables, sun drying them, then deep-frying. Try making Julia's easy-peasy Kripik Kentang Pedas Manis (page 18) using store-bought potato chips.

Then we have deep-fried savory snacks usually served for breakfast, second breakfast, elevenses, or afternoon tea! Pangsit Goreng (page 19) is quick and easy to make, and Kroket Kentang (page 27) may take longer but is worth the effort. Other items might fall into the roti (bread) category. Roti Bakso (page 29), filled with sweet pork and candied winter melon, is one such snack.

Chapter 1
_____

Savory Nibbles
Cemilan

In Indonesia, snacks are sold at supermarkets (the snack sections are ginormous!), as well as at traditional markets and from street vendors where they are called jajanan pasar (market buys).

And, of course, you can make them at home. These snacks make great appetizers for a dinner party, and some like Martabak Telur Mini (page 23) are also filling enough for a light meal. Here, I have included only savory snacks; if you're craving something sweet, turn to Chapter 5.

Sweet and Spicy Potato Chips

KRIPIK KENTANG PEDAS MANIS

Makes 4 servings

3 tablespoons sugar

1 tablespoon sambal oelek

1 tablespoon distilled white vinegar

1 package (5 oz/140 g) unsalted or sea salt thick-cut potato chips, such as Kettle brand

Sweet and spicy tapioca crisps were one of my favorite childhood snacks. These crisps are potato chips' exotic, far-flung cousins shellacked in a sweet, spicy, and tangy coating. I couldn't get enough of them, my taste buds craving more as my fingers popped crisp after crisp into my mouth on autopilot.

Well, a few years ago, Julia learned to make a potato chip version. And, of course, there's a story to go with it! "When Daddy goes to my friend's house, she makes kripik for him, and he finishes everything. He loves this!" she told me. This happened so frequently that finally, in embarrassment, Julia just asked her friend for the recipe.

Kripik kentang uses only four ingredients, and you probably already have them in your pantry—sambal oelek, sugar, vinegar, and store-bought potato chips. My advice: make a double batch and don't bother saving it for tomorrow (or anyone else). They taste best eaten right away anyway.

Combine the sugar, sambal, and vinegar in a wok or large, heavy pot over medium-high heat. Stir constantly until the sugar dissolves and the mixture thickens and starts to bubble, 3–4 minutes. Reduce the heat to low. Taste and adjust the seasonings if desired.

Pour the entire package of chips into the wok and stir gently to coat. The chips should be lightly coated with sauce.

Devour immediately or allow to cool before storing in an airtight container for 1–2 days.

Fried Wontons

PANGSIT GORENG

Makes 45–50 wontons

¾ lb (340 g) ground pork or beef

1 green onion, finely chopped

1 clove garlic, minced

1 teaspoon sesame oil

½ teaspoon fine sea salt

¼ teaspoon ground white
  or black pepper

Vegetable oil for frying

50 (3½-inch/9-cm) square
  wonton wrappers

Julia often made pangsit by wrapping a small amount of seasoned ground meat—usually pork or chicken—in what would appear to be a disproportionately large wonton wrapper. She did this for two reasons: One, so that the meat would be fully cooked before the wrapper burned. And two, because she knew we enjoyed the crispy, crunchy fried wrappers more than the filling itself! They do taste best freshly fried so try to fry them at the very last minute.

Mix together the pork, green onion, garlic, sesame oil, salt, and white pepper in a medium bowl. (To check for seasoning, you can fry a teaspoon in a little vegetable oil and taste.)

To assemble the wontons, have the following within arm's reach: the wrappers covered with a damp cloth, a small bowl of water, and a parchment-lined baking sheet or plate.

Place a wonton wrapper in the palm of your left hand with a corner facing you (it should look like a diamond). Scoop a teaspoon of filling into the center. Dip your index finger in water and paint the top 2 edges of the diamond. Fold the bottom tip over the filling to form a triangle. Press the edges together while pushing out air from the center. Place on the prepared baking sheet and repeat until all the filling is used up.

Heat 1 inch (2.5 cm) of vegetable oil in a small saucepan or skillet over high heat until an instant-read thermometer reads 350°F (180°C). If you don't have a thermometer, fry a small piece of wonton wrapper. If it starts to sizzle, the oil is ready. (See page 200 for deep-frying tips.)

Reduce the heat to medium and gently lower 4–5 wontons into the oil (or as many as will fit), making sure they can float freely. Fry until golden brown on both sides, 45 seconds to 1 minute, flipping halfway through cooking. Scoop up the wontons with a wire mesh strainer or slotted spoon and drain on paper towels or a wire rack. Watch the wontons carefully because they cook—and burn—quickly.

Bring the oil back up to temperature before frying the wontons in batches until they're all done. You can keep them warm in a 250°F (120°C) oven.

Serve immediately with sweet chili sauce. They are also delicious with Bakmi Jamur (page 113).

Curry Puffs

KARIPAP

Fried pastries are a favorite street food snack in Singapore and Indonesia. These curry puffs are the Singapore version filled with curried chicken and potatoes. (The Indonesian version is called pastel goreng and filled with meat, potatoes, and cellophane noodles.) Having lived in Singapore for decades, my family prefers curry puffs. Although Julia used to make her own dough, she now uses store-bought dough, as do I.

In a large bowl, toss the chicken with 1 teaspoon of salt.

Heat the 2 tablespoons oil in a wok or large, heavy skillet over medium heat until shimmering hot. Add the onion and stir and cook until soft, about 30 seconds. Add the curry powder and cayenne, stirring until fragrant, about 1 minute.

Raise the heat to high and add the chicken followed by the potato, stirring to coat with the curry mixture after each addition. Add the coconut milk and water and bring to a boil. Reduce the heat to medium-low, add the sugar and the remaining ½ teaspoon of salt, and simmer until the chicken and potatoes are tender and most of the liquid has evaporated, 10–12 minutes. There will be some oil remaining at the bottom of the pan. Taste and adjust the amount of curry powder, salt, and sugar if desired. Transfer the chicken-potato mixture to a large bowl, draining any liquid, and cool for at least 30 minutes.

To assemble the puffs, lay a wrapper on a dry work surface and place 1 tablespoon filling in the center. Place 1 egg quarter (if using) on top. Fold the bottom edge of the circle over the filling to form a half-moon and firmly press the edges together to seal tightly. Crimp with your fingers.

Heat about 2 inches (5 cm) of oil in a wok or heavy pot over medium-high heat until an instant-read thermometer reads 350°F (180°C). Reduce the heat to medium and gently lower the puffs one at a time into the hot oil. The puffs should float freely and not touch the bottom of the pot, or there will be a dark burn spot. Deep-fry until golden brown, 3–5 minutes, turning as needed for even browning. Transfer the puffs to a wire rack or paper towels. Bring the oil back up to temperature before frying the next batch. Repeat until all the puffs are cooked.

Serve hot or at room temperature.

Makes 10 curry puffs

- ½ lb (225 g) boneless, skinless chicken thighs or breasts, cut into ½-inch (12-mm) dice
- 1½ teaspoons fine sea salt, divided
- 2 tablespoons vegetable oil, plus more for frying
- ¼ small yellow onion, finely chopped
- 1 tablespoon curry powder
- ¼ teaspoon ground cayenne pepper, or to taste
- 1 yellow gold potato, peeled and cut into ½-inch (12-mm) dice
- 3 tablespoons unsweetened coconut milk
- ½ cup (120 ml) water
- 1 teaspoon sugar
- 10 (5-inch/13-cm) round empanada dough wrappers, such as Goya brand
- 3 large hard-boiled eggs, quartered lengthwise (optional)

NOTES
To bake, cut 1 package (1 lb/450 g) puff pastry into 10 squares. Fill each square with 1 tablespoon of filling and fold into a triangle. Crimp the edges with a fork. Brush each puff with egg wash (1 egg + 1 tablespoon milk) and bake in a preheated 400°F (200°C) oven for 15–20 minutes, or until golden brown.

Savory Stuffed Pancakes

MARTABAK TELUR MINI

Makes 10–12 pancakes

FOR THE SAUCE

½ cup (120 ml) water

¼ cup (60 ml) distilled
  white vinegar

2 tablespoons granulated sugar

2 tablespoons shaved palm
  sugar or brown sugar

2 red or green bird's eye
  chilies or Thai chilies,
  seeded (optional),
  stemmed, and chopped

1 Asian shallot, minced

½ English cucumber, diced

¼ teaspoon fine sea salt

3 tablespoons vegetable
  oil, plus more for frying

1 cup (140 g) diced yellow
  onion, divided

2 cloves garlic, minced

4 curry leaves (optional)

2 tablespoons curry powder

½ lb (225 g) ground beef

1 teaspoon fine sea salt

1 teaspoon granulated sugar

3 green onions or
  1 leek, chopped

4 large eggs, beaten

2 tablespoons tapioca
  flour or cornstarch

2 tablespoons water

12 (8-inch/20-cm) square
  spring roll wrappers, plus
  extras in case some tear

In Indonesia, there are two types of martabak. Martabak manis is a sweet yeasted pancake filled with any one or more of the following: chocolate, peanuts, sweet cheese, and condensed milk. Martabak telur, a savory parcel thought to be Middle Eastern in origin, is chock-full of ground beef and egg. Julia's shortcut version uses store-bought spring roll wrappers, and she's happy to use any meat she has on hand.

To make the sauce, bring the water, vinegar, and sugars to a boil in a small pot over high heat. When the sugars have dissolved, remove from the heat and set aside to cool. When the sauce is cool, add the chilies, shallot, cucumber, and salt. Taste and adjust the seasonings. The sauce can be made ahead and refrigerated for up to 5 days.

Heat the oil in a large skillet over medium heat until shimmering hot. Add ¼ cup (35 g) of onion and the garlic and stir and cook until fragrant, about 45 seconds. Add the curry leaves (if using) and curry powder and stir until fragrant, 1–2 minutes. Add the beef. Stir and cook until no longer pink, 2–3 minutes. Season with the salt and sugar and transfer to a large bowl to cool. When the meat has cooled to room temperature, add the remaining ¾ cup (105 g) of onion and the green onions. Mix in the eggs. In a small bowl, combine the tapioca flour and water to create a thick slurry.

To assemble, have the following within arm's reach: the beef filling, the wrappers covered with a damp cloth, tapioca slurry for sealing, and a parchment-lined baking sheet.

Peel off a wrapper and lay it on a dry work surface with the bottom corner pointing toward you like a diamond. Spoon 2 tablespoons of filling in the center. Fold the bottom corner over the filling. Fold the left and right corners in to form an open envelope. Fold over into a rectangular parcel. Seal the edges with slurry and place the parcel seam-side down on the prepared baking sheet. The parcels will measure about 5 inches (13 cm) square. Repeat until all the filling is used up. You may have wrappers left over.

Heat ½ inch (12 mm) of oil in a wok or heavy skillet over medium heat until shimmering hot. Working in batches, slip the parcels seam-side down into the hot oil. Fry until golden brown on both sides, 3–4 minutes, flipping halfway through cooking. Drain on a wire rack or paper towels. Repeat until all the parcels are fried. Serve with sauce on the side.

Fried Spring Rolls

LUMPIA GORENG

Makes 20 spring rolls

2 tablespoons vegetable
oil, plus more for frying

6 Asian shallots or 3 European
shallots, chopped

3 cloves garlic, chopped

½ lb (225 g) ground
pork or chicken

1 can (19 oz/540 g) shredded
bamboo shoots, drained

¼ lb (115 g) raw shrimp, peeled,
deveined, and chopped

1 tablespoon dried shrimp,
soaked in water for
10 minutes, patted dry,
and minced (optional)

3 tablespoons kecap manis

1 tablespoon fish sauce
or soy sauce

1 teaspoon sugar

½ teaspoon fine sea salt

½ teaspoon ground white
or black pepper

¼ cup (15 g) chopped Chinese
celery leaves or parsley

2 green onions, finely chopped

20 (8-inch/20-cm) square
spring roll wrappers, or
any size you can find, such
as Spring Home brand

Sweet and Garlicky Sauce
(recipe follows)

Unlike other spring rolls or egg rolls you might have had, this lumpia from Semarang (a city in Central Java) is stuffed with a bamboo shoot filling. As a little girl, I had to work for my lumpia, and rolling them was one of the first kitchen tasks I learned. Despite all the practice I've had, I still can't fold them as neatly and tightly as Julia can. Oh well, at least they're just as delicious!

Heat the 2 tablespoons of oil in a wok or large, heavy skillet over medium heat until shimmering hot. Add the shallots and garlic and stir and cook until fragrant, about 1 minute. Add the pork and cook until no longer pink, 2–3 minutes.

Add the bamboo shoots, fresh shrimp, and dried shrimp (if using) and stir and cook until the shrimp turn pink, 1–2 minutes. Add the kecap manis, fish sauce, sugar, salt, and white pepper and mix until all the ingredients are well coated. Taste and adjust the seasonings if desired. Add the celery leaves and green onions, give the ingredients a final whirl in the wok, then remove from the heat. Transfer the mixture to a colander placed in the sink or over a bowl to drain and cool completely.

To assemble the lumpia, have the following within arm's reach: the pork filling, the wrappers covered with a damp cloth to keep them moist, a bowl of water for sealing, and a parchment-lined baking sheet to hold the rolled lumpia.

Peel off a wrapper and lay it on a dry work surface like a diamond with the bottom corner pointing toward you. Place 2 tablespoons of filling just below the center line of the wrapper parallel to your body. Fold the bottom corner over the filling and tuck it under. Then fold the left and right sides in to form an envelope. Roll the lumpia tightly into a fat tube. Before you reach the end, dab a little water along the edges and seal completely. The lumpia should measure 4–5 inches (10–13 cm) in length and 1–1½ inches (2.5–4 cm) in diameter. Place seam-side down on the prepared baking sheet. Repeat with remaining filling and wrappers.

Heat 2 inches (5 cm) of oil in a wok or medium heavy pot over high heat until an instant-read thermometer reads 350°F (180°C). (See page 200 for deep-frying tips.)

If you can find fresh bamboo shoots at an Asian market, you will need about 10½ oz (300 g).

Lumpia are best eaten when freshly fried. If left overnight, they get soggy and the wrappers lose their crisp shell. However, you can freeze assembled but uncooked lumpia for up to 1 month. Line them up in a single layer on a baking sheet to prevent them from sticking together and place in the freezer. Once they are frozen, you can store them in a zip-top bag in the freezer. To serve, simply deep-fry them (for an extra minute or so) straight from the freezer.

Reduce the heat to medium and gently lower the lumpia into the oil one at a time, making sure they have room to float freely and don't touch the bottom of the pot. Fry in batches, rolling the lumpia in the oil until both sides are evenly golden brown, 1–2 minutes. Remove the lumpia with a wire mesh strainer, shaking off excess oil, and drain on paper towels or a wire rack.

Bring the oil back up to temperature before frying the next batch. Repeat until all the lumpia are fried. You can keep them warm in a 250°F (120°C) oven.

Serve immediately with Sweet and Garlicky Sauce.

_____

SWEET AND GARLICKY SAUCE

¾ cup (180 ml) water, divided

2 tablespoons sugar

1 tablespoon kecap manis

½ teaspoon salt

2 cloves garlic, minced

4 teaspoons tapioca flour or cornstarch

4–6 red or green bird's eye chilies or Thai chilies, chopped

2 teaspoons distilled white vinegar

Combine ½ cup (120 ml) of water, the sugar, kecap manis, salt, and garlic in a small saucepan over medium heat and bring to a boil, stirring to dissolve the sugar.

In a small bowl, mix together the tapioca flour and remaining ¼ cup (60 ml) of water to create a slurry. Add the slurry to the pan, stirring constantly, until the sauce bubbles and thickens, about 1 minute. The sauce should be the consistency of Thai sweet chili sauce but not as thick as ketchup.

Remove from the heat and add the chilies and vinegar. Taste and adjust the seasonings if desired. Serve with lumpia. Makes ¾ cup (180 ml).

Chicken and Potato Croquettes

KROKET KENTANG

Makes about 24 croquettes

FOR THE FILLING

½ lb (210 g) boneless, skinless chicken thighs or breasts or 1¼ cups leftover cooked chicken

1 lb (450 g) yellow gold potatoes

6 tablespoons (90 g) unsalted butter

6 small Asian shallots or 3 large European, minced

3 cloves garlic, minced

1¼ cups (145 g) all-purpose flour, divided

1 cup (240 ml) + 2 tablespoons whole or 2 percent milk, divided

1 cup (140 g) frozen peas and carrots, thawed

½ cup (30 g) finely chopped Chinese celery leaves or parsley

3 tablespoons sugar

1½ teaspoons ground nutmeg

1 tablespoon fine sea salt

¾ teaspoon ground white or black pepper

FOR ASSEMBLY AND FRYING

1½ cups (150 g) breadcrumbs

2 large eggs, beaten

Vegetable oil for frying

Sambal Kacang I (page 167, optional)

With its creamy center and crisp outer crust, this Dutch-Indonesian snack is a fan favorite! The name kroket comes from the Dutch word *kroketten*. What started off as an elite snack that only the colonists consumed is now an everyday food that can be made using leftovers. There are different fillings too—chicken, beef, and cheese are commonly used. The most popular version of kroket is made by wrapping the filling with a potato "dough," which is then breaded and deep-fried. Julia combines everything, including the potatoes, into one creamy filling instead. I recommend making the filling on one day and breading and deep-frying on another.

To make the filling, poach the chicken (using the method on page 34) and cut into ¼-inch (6-mm) dice.

Boil the potatoes until tender. Peel and cut into ¼-inch (6-mm) dice.

Melt the butter in a wok or large, heavy nonstick skillet over medium-low heat. Once the butter melts, add the shallots and garlic and stir and cook until fragrant, 30–45 seconds. Sprinkle in 1 cup (115 g) of flour and use a wooden spoon to stir in a figure-eight motion until the flour has completely absorbed all the butter, 30 seconds to 1 minute.

Gradually add 1 cup (240 ml) of milk and cook and stir over low heat until the roux thickens into a soft dough, 8–10 minutes. If any lumps of flour remain, break them up with your spoon.

Add the cooked chicken, cooked potatoes, peas and carrots, and celery leaves, mixing in between each addition. Season with the sugar, nutmeg, salt, and white pepper. Add the remaining 2 tablespoons of milk and continue to stir until the "dough" is cooked through, just a little sticky, and firm enough to be rolled into balls, 20–25 minutes. Taste and adjust the seasonings if desired. It should taste sweet, savory, and noticeably nutmeggy. Set aside to cool, then refrigerate for at least 2 hours or up to 3 days.

To assemble, have the following within arm's reach: the cold potato filling, 2 rimmed plates (1 with the remaining ¼ cup [30 g] of flour and 1 with the breadcrumbs), a bowl filled with the beaten eggs, and a parchment-lined baking sheet for the rolled kroket.

To bake, preheat the oven to 400°F (200°C). Place the kroket on a greased baking sheet and brush all sides with oil. Bake for 12–15 minutes, until golden, flipping halfway through cooking.

To air-fry, grease the air fryer basket. Place the kroket in the basket and air fry at 400°F (200°C) for 8–10 minutes, flipping halfway through cooking.

You can make your own bread-crumbs. When we lived in Singapore, Julia would sun stale pieces of bread in the garden. Once they were crusty, she'd pound them with a mortar and pestle until the texture of sand. You can also bake stale bread in a 175°F (80°C) oven for 2 hours to achieve the same effect.

I like using panko, Japanese breadcrumbs with a light, delicate texture that crisps as it cooks. Panko also absorbs less oil than regular breadcrumbs, and food stays crunchy. It has a coarser texture than regular breadcrumbs so pulse them a few times in a food processor or pound with a mortar and pestle. Panko is available in the Asian section of larger supermarkets.

Kroket taste best when freshly fried, but you can refrigerate them for 5 days or freeze for up to 1 month. Warm in a 350°F (180°C) oven for 10 minutes, until crisp on the outside and heated through.

Dust your hands with flour and roll 2 tablespoons of filling into an egg-shaped or round ball. Place on the prepared baking sheet. Repeat until all the filling is used up.

Using separate hands (so the flour doesn't get clumpy from the egg), coat each ball in the flour, the egg, and finally the breadcrumbs. Make sure to cover all surfaces. Return to the baking sheet. Repeat until all the kroket have been breaded.

At this point, you can freeze the kroket on the baking sheet for an hour or two, then tip into a zip-top bag to fry at another time. (Do not thaw before frying and fry for an extra minute or two, adjusting the heat so that the outside doesn't burn before the inside is heated up).

Regardless, I recommend placing the kroket in the freezer to stay firm while the oil heats up.

Heat 2 inches (5 cm) of oil in a wok or medium deep, heavy pot over high heat until an instant-read thermometer reads 350°F (180°C). (See page 200 for deep-frying tips).

Reduce the heat to medium. Using tongs, gently lower the kroket into the hot oil one at a time, making sure they float freely and don't touch the bottom of the pan. Fry in batches until golden brown on all sides, 1–1½ minutes. Nudge the kroket around in the oil as needed so they cook evenly. Remove with a wire mesh straner and drain on a wire rack or paper towels.

Remove any rogue breadcrumbs and bring the oil back up to temperature before frying the next batch. Repeat until all the kroket are fried. You can keep them warm in a 250°F (120°C) oven.

Serve warm or at room temperature with sambal kacang I (if using).

FROM OUR RECIPE TESTERS
Recipe tester Laura McCarthy used a (4-qt/3.7-L) saucepan with 2 inches (5 cm) of oil and fried 5 kroket at a time. "I thought it was perfect, not too big, not at all intimidating with all of that hot oil," she says.

Sweet Pork Buns

ROTI BAKSO

Makes 16 buns

3 cups (370 g) all-purpose flour, plus more as needed

¾ cup (180 ml) + 3 tablespoons warm milk, divided

3 tablespoons water

¼ (50 g) cup sugar

2 teaspoons instant dry yeast

1 teaspoon fine sea salt

4 tablespoons (60 g) unsalted butter, softened

Vegetable oil for greasing

Sweet Pork Filling (recipe follows)

1 large egg and 1 teaspoon water combined into an egg wash

2 tablespoons honey and 2 tablespoons hot water combined into a syrup

Julia's mother, my Poh Poh, bribed Julia and her siblings with roti bakso. Poh Poh told them that if they napped in the afternoon—and only if they fell fast asleep—freshly baked roti bakso would be waiting for them when they woke up. And it worked like a charm! I was such a good kid, I never had to be bribed . . . ha ha. Julia made these buns all the same, and we enjoyed them. While Poh Poh's dough recipe was easy enough, I like using milk bread dough.

Place the flour in a large bowl. Scoop out 2 tablespoons and combine with 3 tablespoons of milk and the water in a small saucepan. Whisk together until no lumps remain. Cook over medium-low heat until bubbles form, then whisk constantly until thick and you can draw a line through the slurry at the bottom of the pan, 2–3 minutes. It will look like mashed potatoes and smell like cooked roux. This is your starter. Set aside to cool until warm to the touch.

Add the sugar, yeast, and salt to the remaining flour in the bowl. Add the starter and the remaining ¾ cup (180 ml) of milk.

If using a stand mixer, mix the flour mixture with a paddle attachment on medium speed, adding the butter, 1 tablespoon at a time, until combined. Switch to a dough hook. Continue mixing on medium-high speed until the dough pulls away from the sides of the bowl and is smooth, elastic, and slightly sticky. Scrape down the sides of the bowl every few minutes. This may take up to 10 minutes.

If kneading by hand, add the butter, 1 tablespoon at a time, mixing with a flexible spatula between each tablespoon, until well combined. Scrape the dough onto a floured surface. If the dough is too wet to knead, gradually add flour, a few tablespoons at a time up to ½ cup (60 g), until you can knead the dough into a loose ball. Continue to knead the dough until smooth and elastic, 20–25 minutes longer.

Rub oil over your hands. Shape the dough into a ball and transfer to a greased bowl. Cover with a damp cloth and set aside to rise in a warm place for 1 hour. (Julia preheats the oven to 200°F/95°C and turns it off. Or if it's sunny, leave it outside.) The dough won't necessarily double in size, but it should be puffy. Punch the dough with your fist. If the indentation remains, the dough is ready.

Recipe continues

Stretch and fold the sides of the dough over to meet in the center. Flip over so the seam is on the bottom. If the dough sticks to your fingers, add more flour a little at a time. Leave for 45 minutes longer until it rises and puffs up again.

Scrape the dough onto a lightly floured surface. Dust your hands with flour and divide the dough into 4 portions, then divide each piece into 4 parts again. You will get 16 portions of about 1½ oz (40 g) each.

Roll each into a ball and pull into a circle about ¼ inch (6 mm) thick and 4 inches (10 cm) in diameter. Place 1 heaping tablespoon of the pork filling in the center, fold over into a half-moon, and pinch the edges to seal. Shape into an oval/football shape with the seam on the bottom. Place on 2 greased baking sheets about 2 inches (5 cm) apart. Cover with a towel and allow to rise for 1 hour.

Preheat the oven to 350°F (180°C) .

Brush each bun with egg wash and bake for 20–25 minutes, or until golden. When the buns come out of the oven, brush with the honey syrup for shine, sweetness, and color.

Serve warm or at room temperature.

SWEET PORK FILLING

1 teaspoon vegetable oil

2 cloves garlic, minced

2 small Asian shallots or 1 large European shallot, minced

½ lb (225 g) ground pork

½ teaspoon fine sea salt

¼ teaspoon ground white or black pepper

2 tablespoons kecap manis

1 green onion, finely chopped

1 tablespoon fried shallots

1 oz (30 g) candied winter melon, finely chopped (optional) (see notes)

Heat the oil in a wok or large, heavy skillet over medium heat until shimmering hot. Add the garlic and shallots and fry until fragrant, 30 seconds to 1 minute. Add the pork, salt, and white pepper and stir and cook until the pork is barely pink, about 2 minutes.

Add the kecap manis, reduce the heat to low, and simmer until the pork is dry and slightly caramelized, about 5 minutes. Remove from the heat and add the green onion and fried shallots. Transfer to a colander and place in the sink or over a bowl to drain and cool completely. Add the candied winter melon (if using) and mix well. Makes about 1 cup (225 g) filling.

Oma says:
When forming the last two to three buns, divide the filling up equally so you won't have any left over.

NOTES
Candied winter melon is sold in plastic packages at Asian markets. It is often arranged in the Tray of Togetherness during Lunar New Year and added to pastry fillings and herbal teas. Candied ginger or coconut might be easier to find and make good substitutes.

Shredded Chicken and Glutinous Rice Dumplings

LEMPER AYAM

Makes 16 dumplings

FOR THE RICE LAYER

2½ cups (490 g) white
   glutinous rice

2½ cups (600 ml) unsweetened
   coconut milk

1 teaspoon salt

2 pandan leaves, knotted,
   or 4 makrut lime leaves

FOR THE FILLING

¾ lb (340 g) boneless, skinless
   chicken breasts or thighs

1½ teaspoons salt, divided

4 candlenuts or unsalted
   macadamia nuts

1 tablespoon coriander seeds
   or ground coriander

1 teaspoon cumin seeds
   or ground cumin

8 Asian shallots or 4 European
   shallots, chopped

4 cloves garlic, smashed

1 teaspoon ground white
   or black pepper

4 tablespoons (60 ml)
   vegetable oil, divided

1 salam leaf or 2 makrut
   lime leaves

1 stalk lemongrass,
   trimmed and bruised

1¼ cups (300 ml) unsweetened
   coconut milk

1 tablespoon Air Asam
   (page 188, optional)

3 tablespoons sugar

16 (8 × 6-inch/20 × 15-cm)
   banana leaf rectangles
   (optional)

Toothpicks or stapler (optional)

Lemper is a snack you can eat on the go. Usually wrapped in banana leaves, it is finger food. Julia would pack them on road trips, and we'd have them for a light lunch or a snack along the way. While it is traditional to steam the lemper in banana leaves, Julia sometimes wraps them in plastic wrap, and I like to wrap them in parchment. Once the layers are put together, wrapping and steaming the lemper isn't necessary, but the steaming does help keep them together. This recipe is best made over a few days.

To make the rice layer, soak the rice in a large bowl with enough water to cover by 2 inches (5 cm) for at least 4 hours and up to 24 hours. Tip the rice into a fine-mesh sieve over another large bowl, shaking to remove excess water, and drain until it stops dripping. Spread the rice out in a 9-inch (23-cm) cake pan, pie plate, or rimmed platter, or the largest size that will fit in your steamer.

Prepare the steamer using the method on page 201.

Reduce the heat to medium and carefully place the cake pan with the drained rice on top of the tray or rack. Steam for 20 minutes. Remove from the heat and wait for the steam to subside. Carefully lift the lid away from you and remove the rice.

While the rice is steaming, combine the coconut milk, salt, and pandan leaves in a small saucepan, then simmer over medium heat for 10 minutes. Do not let it come to a rolling boil.

Remove the pandan leaves and pour the coconut milk over the half-cooked rice. Stir until completely absorbed. (If using a shallow platter, mix the rice with the coconut milk in the saucepan.) Return the rice to the steamer for 20 minutes longer. Remove from the heat and wait for the steam to subside. Carefully lift the lid away from you and test the rice. The rice is cooked when it's translucent and soft. If it seems dry, sprinkle a tablespoon or two of water over the rice and cover for a few minutes to allow it to steam in the residual heat. Once ready, remove from the heat, crack the cover open, and set aside until cool enough to handle.

Recipe continues

When making Opor Ayam Putih (page 56), save ½ cup (120 ml) of sauce and 2 cups (340 g) of finely shredded chicken to prepare lemper ayam. Simmer the sauce and chicken with 3 lime leaves and 2 teaspoons of sugar until the sauce has been completely absorbed by the meat, 10–15 minutes.

To start the filling, place the chicken in a small saucepan with enough water to cover by 1 inch (2.5 cm) and add 1 teaspoon of salt. Bring to a boil over medium-high heat, then reduce the heat and simmer gently until cooked, 15–20 minutes. To check, insert an instant-read thermometer into the thickest part of the chicken; it should read 165°F (74°C). Or insert a knife; the juicecs should run clear. Transfer to a bowl and allow to cool. Save the broth for another use.

When the chicken is cool enough to handle, pull into very fine shreds using your fingers or 2 forks. The chicken should look almost like floss. You will have about 1½ cups (250 g).

While the chicken is cooking, start the spice paste: Toast the candlenuts (5–6 minutes), coriander seeds (5–6 minutes), and cumin seeds (1–2 minutes) separately in a small, dry skillet over medium heat until fragrant and browned. Crush the candlenuts with the flat part of a knife's blade. Grind the coriander and cumin into a coarse powder in a spice grinder or with a mortar and pestle. (If using ground coriander and cumin, just add to the food processor in the next step.)

In a small food processor or blender, pulse the candlenuts, coriander, cumin, shallots, garlic, and white pepper with 1 tablespoon of oil until the texture of oatmeal. Scrape down the sides of the bowl as needed. Or use a mortar and pestle. (If using a mortar and pestle, grind the spices first, then add the rest of the ingredients one by one with a pinch of salt.)

Heat 2 tablespoons of oil in a wok or medium heavy skillet over medium heat until shimmering hot. Add the spice paste, salam leaf, and lemongrass, then stir and cook until fragrant, 5–7 minutes. Reduce the heat if the paste is browning too fast; you don't want it to burn.

Add the coconut milk, air asam (if using), cooked chicken, sugar, and remaining ½ teaspoon of salt, mixing well. Reduce the heat to medium-low and simmer until the meat has completely absorbed the liquid and feels dry to the touch, 15–25 minutes. The filling should be sweet and savory and definitely not soggy. Taste and adjust the seasonings if desired. (The filling can be prepared up to 2 days ahead, covered, and refrigerated.)

Line the sides and bottom of a 9 × 13-inch (23 × 33-cm) baking dish with plastic wrap or parchment paper.

Wear gloves or wet your fingertips so the rice won't stick. Divide the rice into 2 equal portions. Press 1 portion firmly into the bottom of the prepared dish to form an even layer about ½ inch (12 mm) thick. Spread the chicken filling evenly over the rice. Try not to leave any gaps. Spread the remaining portion of rice on top of the chicken and press down firmly. You want the 3 layers (rice, chicken, rice) to stick together and not fall apart when you cut into it. Rub the remaining 1 tablespoon of oil onto a knife and cut into 16 pieces.

Carefully remove the pieces one at a time and mold into about 3 × 1½-inch (7.5 × 4-cm) logs, smoothing the rice over the filling to hide it. Don't worry if there's some peekaboo filling.

You can eat the lemper as is, or wrap them in banana leaves for easy transport.

To use the banana leaves, put a leaf rectangle on a dry work surface with the smooth, dark-green side up and the longer side parallel to your body. Place the lemper in the center of the leaf. Taking the edge closest to you, fold the leaf over the lemper and roll into a bundle until you reach the end of the leaf. You can trim the ends to make it neater. Secure each end with a toothpick or staple.

Prepare the steamer and arrange the wrapped lemper on the steamer rack. Steam for 4–6 minutes, until the packets are soft and heated through. Turn off the heat and wait for the steam to subside. Carefully lift the lid away from you and remove the lemper.

Serve warm or at room temperature. To eat, unwrap one side and bite into the lemper.

FROM OUR RECIPE TESTERS
"The chicken filling flavor was so outstanding," says recipe tester Debra Samuels. "The whole dish was amazing. What a spectacular combination of flavors. The chicken filling could stand on its own with a bowl of rice." Debra also suggests using ground chicken. And why not?

Indonesians, like many other Asian cultures, often eat family style, what we call makan tengah, or "eat in the middle." There is usually a staple, most often rice but maybe corn or cassava, and an assortment of dishes in the center of the table. Everyone helps themselves to the various dishes and composes a personal meal.

When I was growing up, dinner was the one meal we shared together as a family. Julia would set a big bowl of rice on the table accompanied by a soup, vegetables, and/or protein—perhaps fish, chicken, or tofu. The dishes varied by cooking methods—deep-fried, boiled, curried, grilled, or stewed—to achieve a blend of flavors and textures. We'd take turns scooping rice onto our plates and then help ourselves to the side dishes. We would usually eat with a fork and spoon and sometimes our fingers. Soups were either ladled into small bowls or directly onto the rice. Like clockwork, sambal, kecap manis, and some crispy krupuk (crackers) would also appear.

Chapter 2
_____

Eat in the Middle
Makan Tengah

Keep in mind that the recipes in this chapter are meant to serve four to six people as part of a multicourse meal (rice plus three to four side dishes), and they are not meals unto themselves. While certain dishes are often matched with others, I won't tell you that you can only eat Ayam Goreng Kuning (page 51) with Sayur Asam (page 43). If you'd like to have Sayur Lodeh (page 44) and Babi Kecap (page 62), go for it. If the flavors don't clash on your tongue, why not mix and match?

Soups and Soto

Soups are usually eaten as a side dish or eaten solo poured over a big bowl of rice for a light lunch. In the Indonesian lexicon, there are two types of dishes we might call soup in English. Soto (also called coto and sroto) and sup. Two things distinguish soto from sup: First, soto tends to be richly spiced and can be clear (Soto Ayam, page 39) or made cloudy with coconut milk (Soto Babat, page 48). Sup is almost always brothy and clear (for example, Sup Buntut, page 47). And second, soto is an Indonesian original, in contrast to the sup dishes that are Dutch or European influenced.

To make the soups in this chapter, homemade stock is ideal. A typical Indonesian stock contains a mix of bones (off-cuts like chicken feet and neck are common), bone-in meat, garlic, onions, Chinese celery, and/or ginger. Simply simmer these ingredients with water on the stove top for an hour or two. If you must, buy a store-bought product that's sodium-free or low in sodium and doesn't contain herbs and seasonings foreign to Indonesian cooking, such as rosemary and celery seed.

Turmeric-Spiced Chicken Soup

SOTO AYAM

Makes 4 servings as a main or 6-8 servings as part of a multicourse meal

FOR THE SPICE PASTE

3 candlenuts or unsalted macadamia nuts

1 teaspoon coriander seeds or ground coriander

2 teaspoons ground turmeric

6 Asian shallots or 3 European shallots, coarsely chopped

3 cloves garlic, smashed

Thumb-size piece fresh ginger, peeled and coarsely chopped

3 tablespoons vegetable oil, divided

2 lb (1 kg) bone-in, skin-on chicken thighs, legs, or breasts

8 cups (1.9 L) water

3 teaspoons fine sea salt, divided

1 teaspoon sugar

½ teaspoon ground white or black pepper

5 makrut lime leaves

2 stalks lemongrass, trimmed and bruised

2 yellow gold potatoes, peeled and cut into ¾-inch (2-cm) cubes

Soto ayam is probably one of the most popular of all the sotos—hearty, heavily spiced soups that are Indonesian originals. There are many variations of this dish across the archipelago, some served with koya (a powder made with shrimp chips and fried garlic) or potato cutlets, but the majority seem to be a riff off Julia's recipe. I'm not sure whether it's soto Lamongan or soto Madura, so let's just say it's Julia's chicken soto. And it's quite delicious. Soto ayam is usually served as a main meal, but you can also enjoy it as a first course or as a soup on the side.

To make the spice paste, toast the candlenuts and coriander seeds separately in a small, dry skillet over medium heat until fragrant and browned, 5-6 minutes each. Smash the candlenuts with the flat part of a knife's blade. Grind the coriander into a coarse powder with a spice grinder or mortar and pestle. (If using ground coriander, just add it to the food processor in the next step.)

In a small food processor or blender, pulse the candlenuts, coriander, turmeric, shallots, garlic, and ginger with 1 tablespoon of oil until the texture of oatmeal, about 1 minute. Scrape down the sides of the bowl as necessary. Or use a mortar and pestle. (If using a mortar and pestle, grind the coriander first, then add the rest of the ingredients one by one with a pinch of salt.)

Heat the remaining 2 tablespoons of oil in a wok or large, heavy pot over medium heat until shimmering hot. Add the spice paste and stir and cook until it is very fragrant and has turned a few shades darker (this indicates the shallots are caramelizing), 5-7 minutes. Reduce the heat if the paste is browning too fast; you don't want the paste to burn. Once the moisture has evaporated, the ingredients will separate from the oil. The paste is now ready for the next step.

Recipe continues

½ lb (225 g) cellophane noodles, soaked in boiling water for 10 minutes until soft

4 large hard-boiled eggs, peeled and quartered

2 cups (180 g) bean sprouts

2 green onions, chopped

1½ cups (150 g) crushed plain or sea salt potato chips

¼ cup (15 g) fried shallots

¼ cup (15 g) chopped Chinese celery leaves or parsley

2 Persian limes, cut into wedges

Sambal oelek for serving

Kecap manis for serving

NOTES

You can substitute rice vermicelli for the cellophane noodles, or simply omit the noodles and eat the soup with rice.

Add the chicken and stir to coat with the spice paste. Pour in the water and add 2 teaspoons of salt, the sugar, and white pepper. Add the lime leaves and lemongrass. Cover and bring to a boil over high heat. Reduce the heat to medium and simmer for 30–40 minutes. (Or cook in an electric pressure cooker on high for 20 minutes and do a natural release.) Insert an instant-read thermometer into the thickest part of the chicken. It should read at least 165°F (74°C). If not, cover and cook for a few minutes longer.

Use tongs or a large slotted spoon to transfer the chicken to a large bowl. It may come apart so go slow and be gentle. When you can comfortably handle the chicken, remove the meat and skin from the bones and shred using 2 forks or cut into bite-size pieces.

Remove and discard the lime leaves and lemongrass. Spoon off as much fat as possible from the surface of the soup or use a fat separator. (You can make the soup the day before and refrigerate. The fat will solidify on the surface and will be easier to remove.)

Add the potatoes to the soup and simmer over medium heat until tender, 10–15 minutes. Taste and add the remaining 1 teaspoon of salt and adjust the seasonings if desired.

To assemble the bowls, divide the noodles, potatoes, egg quarters, bean sprouts, and chicken among 4 bowls. Pour ¾–1 cup (180–240 ml) of piping hot soup into each bowl and garnish with the green onions, potato chips, fried shallots, and celery leaves. Serve immediately with lime wedges, sambal, and kecap manis in little dishes. My family eats soto ayam with a side of rice to make it a full meal.

Oma says:

You will probably have chicken meat left over. Use it to make Kroket Kentang (page 27), or Pastel Panggang (page 114).

Tamarind Vegetable Soup

SAYUR ASAM

Makes 4 servings as a main or 6–8 servings as part of a multicourse meal

6 Asian shallots or
  3 European shallots

3 cloves garlic, smashed

2 medium-hot long red chilies,
  such as Fresno or cayenne,
  seeded (optional) and chopped

1 teaspoon Terasi Bakar
  (page 189) or anchovy
  paste (optional)

1½ teaspoons fine sea
  salt, divided

4 cups (950 ml) water

1 cup (240 ml) Air
  Asam (page 188)

3 salam leaves or makrut
  lime leaves

2 (½-inch/12-mm)
  galangal slices

2 ears fresh corn, each cut
  crosswise into 4–5 pieces

1 chayote, peeled, seeded, and
  cut into 1-inch (2.5-cm) pieces

6 oz (170 g) yard-long beans
  or green beans, cut into
  2-inch (5-cm) pieces

1 can (20 oz/570 g) young
  jackfruit in brine, drained,
  hard bottom stem removed
  (reserve for making Gudeg,
  page 101), fruit cut into
  1-inch (2.5-cm) pieces

½ cup (90 g) cooked red beans
  (azuki or kidney), pinto beans,
  or boiled peanuts

4–6 tablespoons sugar

This soup is not strictly vegetarian (like many Indonesian vegetable and tofu dishes) because it includes shrimp paste. You can omit it, but I think a crucial component of the soup's flavor profile will be lost. If you can't find chayote, use zucchini, green papaya, or kohlrabi. Although Julia flavors this soup with salam leaves and galangal, you can substitute ginger, lemongrass, and/or makrut lime leaves.

To make the spice paste, pulse the shallots, garlic, chilies, terasi bakar (if using), and ½ teaspoon of salt in a small food processor or blender until the texture of oatmeal, about 1 minute. Scrape down the sides of the bowl as needed. Or use a mortar and pestle.

Combine the water, air asam, spice paste, salam leaves, and galangal in a large pot and bring to a boil over high heat. Reduce the heat to medium, add the corn and chayote, and simmer until half-cooked, 5–7 minutes.

Add the yard-long beans, jackfruit, and red beans, then stir in the remaining 1 teaspoon of salt and the sugar. Cook until the vegetables are tender or cooked to your liking, 3–5 minutes. Taste and adjust the seasonings if desired. The soup is supposed to be sweet and tart (more sweet if you're Julia!).

Set the soup aside for at least 1 hour to allow the flavors to meld. Serve with steamed rice and Ayam Goreng Kuning (page 51).

FROM OUR RECIPE TESTERS
"It was interesting that a soup could be both hearty and light! Very healthful," says recipe tester Debra Samuels.

Vegetables in Coconut Milk

SAYUR LODEH

Makes 4 servings as a main or 6-8 servings as a side

FOR THE SPICE PASTE

3 candlenuts or unsalted macadamias

1 teaspoon coriander seeds or ground coriander

6 Asian shallots or 3 European shallots, chopped

3 cloves garlic, smashed

2 medium-hot finger-length red chilies, such as Fresno, cayenne, or serrano, seeded (optional) and chopped, or 1 tablespoon sambal oelek

1 tablespoon dried shrimp, soaked in water for 10 minutes and patted dry (optional)

3 tablespoons vegetable oil, divided

2 cups (475 ml) unsweetened coconut milk

1 chayote, peeled, seeded, and cut into bite-size pieces

1 Chinese or Japanese eggplant, cut into bite-size pieces

¼ lb (115 g) green beans, trimmed and cut into 2-inch (5-cm) lengths

¼ lb (115 g) firm tofu or tempeh, cut into 1-inch (2.5-cm) cubes

4 salam leaves or makrut lime leaves

2 (½-inch/12-mm) slices galangal or fresh ginger

1 stalk lemongrass, trimmed and bruised

1 teaspoon fine sea salt

¼ teaspoon ground pepper

½ teaspoon sugar

Fried shallots for serving

Sayur lodeh is one dish that easily flits between everyday and festive occasions. Some people may enjoy it for breakfast, while others serve it at big celebrations like weddings and birthdays. Julia serves it as a side dish for dinner or as part of a festive meal to celebrate the fifteenth day of the Lunar New Year. The spread is collectively dubbed Lontong Cap Go Meh (see page 183).

To make the spice paste, toast the candlenuts and coriander seeds separately in a small, dry skillet over medium heat until fragrant and browned, 5–6 minutes each. Smash the candlenuts with the flat part of a knife's blade. Grind the coriander into a coarse powder with a spice grinder or mortar and pestle.

In a small food processor or blender, pulse the candlenuts, coriander, shallots, garlic, chilies, and dried shrimp (if using) with 1 tablespoon of oil until the texture of oatmeal, about 1 minute. Scrape down the sides of the bowl as necessary. Or use a mortar and pestle.

Heat the remaining 2 tablespoons of oil in a wok or large, heavy pot over medium heat until shimmering hot. Add the spice paste and stir and cook until it is very fragrant and has turned a few shades darker (this indicates the shallots are caramelizing), 5–7 minutes. Reduce the heat if the paste is browning too fast; you don't want the paste to burn. Once the moisture has evaporated, the ingredients will separate from the oil. The paste is now ready for the next step.

Stir in the coconut milk and 2 cups (475 ml) water. Add the chayote, eggplant, green beans, and tofu and bring to a boil, adding more water to cover the vegetables if necessary. Add the salam leaves, galangal, and lemongrass. Reduce the heat to low and simmer, covered, until the chayote and eggplant are tender, 10–12 minutes. Stir in the salt, white pepper, and sugar. Taste and adjust the seasonings if desired. Set the soup aside for 1–2 hours so the flavors can meld.

Sprinkle with fried shallots and serve with steamed rice or Lontong (page 182) as a main meal or in small bowls as a side dish.

Oxtail Soup

SUP BUNTUT

Makes 4 servings as a main meal served with rice

1½ lb (680 g) oxtails

2 whole cloves

1-inch (2.5-cm) cinnamon stick

3 makrut lime leaves (optional)

6 Asian shallots or 3 European shallots, chopped

3 cloves garlic, smashed

2½ teaspoons salt, divided

1 tablespoon unsalted butter

1 tablespoon vegetable oil

2 carrots, chopped

2 yellow gold potatoes, peeled and cut into bite-size pieces

1 teaspoon sugar

½ teaspoon ground white or black pepper

¼ teaspoon ground nutmeg

3 large green cabbage leaves, chopped

1 large Roma tomato, chopped

FOR SERVING

Chopped Chinese celery leaves or parsley

Chopped green onions

Fried shallots

Fried garlic (optional)

Steamed rice

Kecap manis

I don't eat much red meat, but Julia's oxtail soup is one dish I cannot resist. Sup buntut is a hand-me-down recipe from the Dutch, a reflection of a more refined and expensive colonial palate. Oxtails are indeed expensive—in Indonesia and even here in the United States. So this isn't a dish Julia or I prepare often. However, my recipe tester Niki Stojnic has tried making it with beef stew meat, and she says the dish comes out just as tasty and hearty! This dish comes together very easily but simmering the oxtails until they're fall-off-the-bone tender does take time. To save time, cook them in an electric pressure cooker for 45 minutes on high pressure.

Bring a large pot of water to a rolling boil over high heat. Estimate enough water to cover the oxtails by 1 inch (2.5 cm). Reduce the heat to medium and add the oxtails, plus more water if necessary.

Parboil the oxtails for 10 minutes. Drain and rinse the oxtails with cold running water to remove any impurities. Clean the pot thoroughly and refill with 10 cups (2.5 L) water. Return the oxtails to the pot and add the cloves, cinnamon stick, and lime leaves (if using). Cover and cook the oxtails over medium-low heat until soft and fall-off-the-bone tender, skimming off any impurities, 2½–3 hours.

While the oxtails are simmering, make the spice paste: Pulse the shallots, garlic, and ½ teaspoon of salt in a small food processor or blender for about 30 seconds. Or grind with a mortar and pestle.

Heat the butter and oil in a small skillet over medium heat and fry the spice paste until fragrant and light golden, 2–3 minutes. Add to the soup.

When the oxtails are tender—check at about 2½ hours—add the carrots and potatoes. Add the remaining 2 teaspoons of salt, the sugar, white pepper, and nutmeg. Raise the heat to medium-high and simmer until the vegetables are tender, about 15 minutes. Add the cabbage leaves and tomato and cook to your liking—I like my cabbage still crunchy, 1–2 minutes. Remove from the heat and taste. Adjust the seasonings if desired.

Ladle the oxtails and vegetables into individual bowls and sprinkle with celery leaves, green onions, fried shallots, and fried garlic (if using). Serve with steamed rice and kecap manis.

Creamy Beef and Tripe Soup

SOTO BABAT

Makes 4–6 servings as part of a multicourse meal

2 tablespoons + 2 teaspoons fine sea salt, divided

1 lb (450 g) cleaned honeycomb tripe, soaked in water for 10 minutes (see notes)

1 lb (450 g) boneless beef brisket or cross-cut beef shank, cut into ½-inch (12-mm) cubes

4 (¼-inch/6-mm) slices fresh ginger

2 salam leaves or bay leaves (optional)

1 stalk lemongrass, trimmed and bruised

4 makrut limes leaves

2 (½-inch/12-mm) slices galangal

3 candlenuts or unsalted macadamias

1 teaspoon coriander seeds or ground coriander

10 Asian shallots or 5 European shallots, chopped

5 cloves garlic, smashed

2 tablespoons vegetable oil, divided

½ lb (225 g) daikon radish, cut into half-moons

1 cup (240 ml) unsweetened coconut milk

1 teaspoon sugar

1 teaspoon ground white or black pepper

I'm not usually a fan of innards, but I will eat tripe when Julia cooks it. Yes, her soto babat is that good. Even my husband was won over. He's ordered tripe dishes at restaurants but none taste as good as Julia's.

So what exactly is tripe? It's the edible stomach walls of ruminant animals. Before you pooh-pooh the idea of eating tripe, here are two good reasons: Tripe is a complete source of protein and is packed with vitamins and minerals. (It is high in cholesterol though!) Plus, purchasing tripe supports nose-to-tail consumption, cutting down on food waste.

Tripe is tough, and the key to a delicious dish is to cook it for several hours using a moist heat method, such as boiling or stewing. They are ideal for tripe's chewy texture and mild taste, making it soft and allowing it to absorb the flavor of fellow ingredients in the pot.

Bring a large pot of water to a rolling boil over high heat. Estimate enough water to cover the tripe by 1 inch (2.5 cm). Reduce the heat to medium and add 2 tablespoons of salt and the tripe, plus more water if necessary. Simmer for 15 minutes. Drain and rinse the tripe in cool water. Cut into 1 × ½-inch (2.5 cm × 12-mm) pieces.

Rinse the pot and add the tripe and beef, followed by 8 cups (1.9 L) water, the ginger, salam leaves (if using), lemongrass, lime leaves, and galangal. Bring to a boil over high heat. Reduce the heat to medium and simmer, covered, until the tripe and beef are soft, 1–1½ hours. Or pressure cook in an electric pressure cooker on high for 30 minutes and release naturally. Drain and set aside. (This step can be done up to 3 days ahead. Refrigerate the tripe and beef until ready to use.)

While the meat is simmering, make the spice paste. Toast the candlenuts and coriander seeds separately in a small, dry, heavy skillet over medium heat until fragrant and browned, 5–6 minutes each. Smash the candlenuts with the flat part of a knife's blade. Grind the coriander into a coarse powder with a spice grinder or mortar and pestle. (If using ground coriander, just add it to the food processor in the next step.)

In a small food processor or blender, pulse the candlenuts, coriander, shallots, and garlic with 1 tablespoon of oil until the texture of oatmeal, about 1 minute. Scrape down the sides of the bowl as necessary. Or use a mortar and pestle. (If using a mortar and pestle, grind the coriander first, then add the rest of the ingredients one by one with a pinch of salt.)

Fried shallots

Chopped Chinese celery
  leaves or parsley

4 Roma tomatoes, cut
  into wedges

Steamed rice

Kecap manis

Sambal Soto (page 166)

Key lime or calamansi
  lime wedges

Emping (melinjo nut
  crackers) (optional)

NOTES

My local Asian market carries
two types of tripe: blanket, or
flat, tripe and honeycomb tripe.
I prefer the latter.

Tripe sold at the Asian market
or butcher has typically already
been cleaned. It should be a pale
cream/white and not greenish or
gray. Soak in cold water for about
10 minutes, and it's ready for the
next steps.

My recipe tester Suzana Dharma
suggests adding tendon to
the soup.

Heat the remaining 1 tablespoon of oil in a small skillet over medium heat until shimmering hot. Add the spice paste and stir and cook until golden brown and fragrant, 2 to 3 minutes. Set aside.

When the tripe and beef are soft, skim off any impurities from the broth (or strain with a fine-mesh sieve if easier). Then add the spice paste and radish to the soup. Simmer over medium heat until the radish is tender, about 15 minutes.

Pour in the coconut milk and season with the remaining 2 teaspoons of salt, the sugar, and white pepper. Taste and adjust the seasonings if desired. Cook until heated through. Fish out the whole herbs and spices and discard.

Pour the soup into individual bowls and garnish with shallots, celery leaves, and tomato wedges. Serve with steamed rice and kecap manis, sambal soto, lime wedges, and emping (if using) on the side.

Poultry

In Southeast Asia, we often ate a breed of chicken called ayam kampung, literally "village chicken." These birds were—and still are—raised in rural areas and are what we might call free-range. They tend to be smaller and leaner than commercial breeds, and today, they fetch a higher price.

When Julia owned her restaurant, she used Cornish game hens to make her famous fried chicken. Store-bought chickens were too big and rubbery for her taste. That being said, organic chickens are a good substitute for ayam kampung, but they are not always affordable. Instead, I look for all-natural, air-chilled chickens weighing 3–4 lb (1.4–1.8 kg) that are not injected with solution.

Turmeric Fried Chicken

AYAM GORENG KUNING

Makes 4-6 servings as part of a multicourse meal

FOR THE SPICE PASTE

8 candlenuts or unsalted macadamias

1 tablespoon coriander seeds or ground coriander

3 cloves garlic, smashed

2 Asian shallots or 1 European shallot, coarsely chopped

1 small yellow onion, chopped

1 medium-hot finger-length red chili, such as Fresno, cayenne, or serrano, seeded (optional) and chopped

2 tablespoons ground turmeric

6 tablespoons (90 ml) vegetable oil, divided

2 stalks lemongrass, trimmed and bruised

4 salam leaves (optional)

4 (½-inch/12-mm) slices galangal or 4 (¼-inch/6-mm) slices fresh ginger

2 tablespoons fine sea salt

1 tablespoon sugar

1 teaspoon ground white or black pepper

3 lb (1.4 kg) chicken legs, thighs and drumsticks separated, or 1 (3–4 lb/1.4–1.8 kg) chicken, cut into 8 parts

1 cup (240 ml) water

Vegetable oil for frying

Ayam goreng kuning is sometimes called ayam goreng ungkep, literally "braised fried chicken." The chicken is first braised in aromatic spices and herbs before frying to a golden-brown finish. Like Ayam Goreng Manis (page 58), this is a two-step recipe, which may seem daunting at first. Just do what Julia does and make this dish over two days. On the first day, braise the chicken and on the next, fry it. In fact, this is a great make-ahead dish. Braise large batches of chicken (the recipe is easily scaled up or down), drain off the marinade, then portion the cooked chicken into freezer bags. During the next few weeks, simply thaw single bags and deep-fry for a quick and easy weeknight meal.

To make the spice paste, toast the candlenuts and coriander seeds separately in a small, dry skillet over medium heat until fragrant and browned, 5–6 minutes each. Crush the candlenuts with the flat part of a knife's blade. Grind the coriander into a coarse powder with a spice grinder or mortar and pestle. (If using ground coriander, just add it to the food processor in the next step.)

In a small food processor or blender, pulse the candlenuts, coriander, garlic, shallots, onion, chili, and turmeric with 3 tablespoons of oil until the texture of oatmeal, about 1 minute. Scrape down the sides of the bowl as necessary. Or use a mortar and pestle. (If using a mortar and pestle, grind the coriander first, then add the rest of the ingredients one by one with a pinch of salt.)

Heat the remaining 3 tablespoons of oil in a wok or Dutch oven over medium heat until shimmering hot. Add the spice paste, lemongrass, salam leaves (if using), and galangal, and stir and cook until it is very fragrant and has turned a few shades darker (this indicates the shallots are caramelizing), 5–7 minutes. Reduce the heat if the paste is browning too fast; you don't want the paste to burn. Once the moisture has evaporated, the ingredients will separate from the oil. The paste is now ready for the next step.

Add the salt, sugar, and white pepper, then add the chicken and stir to coat. Pour in the water. The liquid should come halfway up the chicken. Add more water if necessary. Stir until the chicken is evenly colored and bring to a gentle boil.

Recipe continues

NOTES

If deep-frying intimidates you, you can also broil, grill, or air-fry the chicken after completing the first step.

Reduce the heat to low and simmer, covered, until the chicken absorbs about half the marinade and is tender and cooked through, 45 minutes to 1 hour. Test the chicken for doneness by cutting into the meat near the bone. Stir occasionally so the chicken doesn't stick to the bottom of the pan.

At this point, the chicken can sit in the marinade in the refrigerator for a day or up to 3 days. In fact, we encourage it! Allow to cool before sealing in a container. If freezing, drain the marinade before storing.

If the chicken is previously frozen or chilled, thaw ahead of time and/or allow to come to room temperature. Prepare a paper towel–lined plate or a wire rack.

Heat about 2 inches (5 cm) of oil in a wok or Dutch oven (4 qt/3.7 L) over high heat until an instant-read thermometer reads 375°F (190°C) on an instant-read thermometer. (See page 200 for deep-frying tips.)

When the oil is hot, reduce the heat to medium. Use tongs to pick up the chicken pieces and shake off excess marinade. Fry the chicken pieces in batches, lowering them gently into the hot oil, until nicely golden brown, about 1 minute. The chicken is already cooked so all you're doing is browning the skin. Drain on the paper towels or wire rack.

Bring the oil back up to temperature before frying the next batch.

Serve with steamed rice and a vegetable side dish.

Smashed Chicken with Green Sambal

AYAM PENYET SAMBAL CABE HIJAU

Makes 4 servings as part of a multicourse meal

FOR THE SPICE PASTE

2 teaspoons coriander seeds or ground coriander

4 Asian shallots or 2 European shallots, chopped

2 cloves garlic, smashed

1 teaspoon fine sea salt

Pinch ground white or black pepper

2 tablespoons vegetable oil, divided

1 lb (450 g) boneless, skinless chicken thighs, cut into 1-inch (2.5-cm) cubes

Sambal Cabe Hijau (page 171) for serving

Green chili sambal scared me when I was little. It just looked so spicy! However, I was recently reintroduced to it, and the sweet, spicy, earthy flavors of the sambal paired with the chicken was a revelation. Eaten with rice, it makes for a simple yet delicious meal. It's also tasty as a taco filling! Ayam penyet is traditionally made with a mortar and pestle. The first step is to pound the sambal into a paste. Then add the cooked chicken and pound, or penyet, the chicken on both sides with the pestle so the chicken absorbs the flavor of the sambal. And it's done!

To make the spice paste, toast the coriander seeds in a small, dry skillet over medium heat until fragrant and browned, 5–6 minutes. Grind into a coarse powder with a spice grinder or mortar and pestle. (If using ground coriander, just add to the food processor in the next step.)

In a small food processor or blender, pulse the coriander, shallots, garlic, salt, and white pepper with 1 tablespoon of oil until the texture of oatmeal, about 1 minute. Scrape down the sides of the bowl as necessary. Or use a mortar and pestle. (If using a mortar and pestle, grind the coriander first, then add the rest of the ingredients one by one with a pinch of salt.)

In a bowl, toss the chicken with the spice paste and marinate for 20 minutes.

Heat the remaining 1 tablespoon of oil in a wok or large, heavy skillet over medium-high heat until shimmering hot. Add the chicken and stir and cook until cooked through and a little crisp on the edges, 6–8 minutes. Cut into a piece to check that it's no longer pink. Drain on a wire rack or paper towels.

Place the sambal in a wide, sturdy bowl and add the chicken. Mash lightly with a potato masher, then mix until the chicken is well coated.

Serve with steamed rice and a vegetable side dish.

Chicken Braised in Coconut Milk and Spices

OPOR AYAM PUTIH

Makes 4-6 servings as part of a multicourse meal

FOR THE SPICE PASTE

5 candlenuts or unsalted macadamias

1 tablespoon coriander seeds or ground coriander

8 Asian shallots or 4 European shallots, chopped

4 cloves garlic, smashed

1 teaspoon ground cumin

1 teaspoon ground white or black pepper

4 tablespoons (60 ml) vegetable oil, divided

1 (3–4 lb/1.4–1.8 kg) chicken, cut into 8 parts

3 salam leaves or makrut lime leaves

2 (½-inch/12-mm) slices galangal

1 stalk lemongrass, trimmed and bruised

3 slices dried kencur, soaked, or ½ teaspoon ground kencur (optional)

2 cups (475 ml) water

2 cups (475 ml) unsweetened coconut milk, divided

1½ tablespoons fine sea salt

1 tablespoon sugar

Fried shallots for serving

Oma says:

Sneak Terasi Bakar (page 189) into this dish to pump up the flavor!

There are two kinds of opor—a white version called opor putih and its yellow counterpart, opor kuning (made with turmeric). Both are popular dishes served during special celebrations like Lebaran (Eid al-Fitr) and selamatan (page 178). Julia has always made opor putih and I tell people it's just like Thai green curry.

To make the spice paste, toast the candlenuts and coriander seeds separately in a small, dry skillet over medium heat until fragrant and browned, 5-6 minutes. Crush the candlenuts with the flat part of a knife's blade. Grind the coriander into a coarse powder with a spice grinder or mortar and pestle.

In a small food processor or blender, pulse the candlenuts, coriander, shallots, garlic, cumin, and pepper with 2 tablespoons of oil until the texture of oatmeal, about 1 minute. Scrape down the sides of the bowl as necessary. Or use a mortar and pestle.

Heat the remaining 2 tablespoons of oil in a large wok or Dutch oven over medium heat until shimmering hot. Add the spice paste and stir and cook until it is very fragrant and has turned a few shades darker (this indicates the shallots are caramelizing), 5-7 minutes. Reduce the heat if the paste is browning too fast; you don't want the paste to burn. Once the moisture has evaporated, the ingredients will separate from the oil. The paste is now ready for the next step.

Add the chicken pieces, salam leaves, galangal, lemongrass, and kencur (if using). Toss to coat the chicken with the spice paste. Stir in the water and bring to a boil.

Reduce the heat to medium-low and add 1 cup (240 ml) of coconut milk followed by the salt and sugar. Cover and simmer until the chicken is tender and cooked through, about 1 hour. Add the remaining 1 cup (240 ml) of coconut milk and stir continuously for about 2 minutes. Taste and adjust the seasonings if desired. Set aside for about 2 hours so that the flavors can meld.

Shower with fried shallots and serve with rice and a vegetable side dish, or as part of Lontong Cap Go Meh (page 183)

NOTES
While this recipe is the OG version, I've also riffed on it by using a whole chicken and cooking it in the oven, serving it with noodles, and adding vegetables like eggplant and zucchini.

Sweet Fried Chicken

AYAM GORENG MANIS

Makes 4-6 servings as part of a multicourse meal

FOR THE SPICE PASTE

3 candlenuts or unsalted macadamias

1 heaping tablespoon coriander seeds or ground coriander

8 Asian shallots or 4 European shallots, chopped

4 cloves garlic, smashed

4 tablespoons (60 ml) vegetable oil, divided

1 (3–4 lb/1.4–1.8 kg) chicken, cut into parts, or 4–6 chicken legs, thighs and drumsticks separated

4 salam leaves or makrut lime leaves

4 (½-inch/12-mm) slices galangal

2 cups (475 ml) coconut water

⅔ cup (100 g) shaved palm sugar or brown sugar

¼ cup (50 g) granulated sugar

1 tablespoon tamarind pulp mixed with ½ cup (120 ml) hot water, or 3 tablespoons store-bought tamarind concentrate

1½ teaspoons fine sea salt, divided

Vegetable oil for frying

Ayam goreng manis is my absolute favorite fried chicken dish! It uses a Central Javanese cooking technique called bacem or baceman. First, the food is braised with herbs, spices, coconut water, and palm sugar until the simmering liquid is reduced and the seasonings are fully absorbed. The sweetness from the palm sugar and the sweet, woodsy coriander undertones infuse the chicken with unmistakable flavor. The second step involves deep-frying or pan-frying. It may seem like a lot of work, but this cooking method has its advantages. Once the first step is done, you can refrigerate (or freeze up to a month) and then deep-fry the chicken in small batches as needed throughout the week. It's such a brilliant make-ahead concept that I think this dish deserves to be called "smart fried chicken"!

To make the spice paste, toast the candlenuts and coriander seeds separately in a small, dry skillet over medium heat until fragrant and browned, 5–6 minutes each. Smash the candlenuts with the flat part of a knife's blade. Grind the coriander into a coarse powder with a spice grinder or mortar and pestle. (If using ground coriander, just add it to the food processor in the next step.)

In a small food processor or blender, pulse the candlenuts, coriander, shallots, garlic, and ½ teaspoon salt with 2 tablespoons of oil until the texture of oatmeal, about 1 minute. Scrape down the sides of the bowl as necessary. Or use a mortar and pestle. (If using a mortar and pestle, grind the coriander first, then add the rest of the ingredients one by one with a pinch of salt.)

Heat the remaining 2 tablespoons of oil in a wok or Dutch oven over medium heat until shimmering hot. Add the spice paste and stir and cook until it is very fragrant and has turned a few shades darker (this indicates the shallots are caramelizing), 5–7 minutes. Reduce the heat if the paste is browning too fast; you don't want the paste to burn. Once the moisture has evaporated, the ingredients will separate from the oil. The paste is now ready for the next step.

Add the chicken and stir to coat with the spice paste. Add the salam leaves, galangal, coconut water, palm and granulated sugars, tamarind, and 1½ teaspoons of salt. The liquid should come halfway up the chicken. Add more coconut water or water if necessary. Stir until the chicken is evenly colored and bring to a gentle boil.

If deep-frying intimidates you, you can also broil, grill, or air-fry the chicken after completing the first step.

If you can't find coconut water, use 2 cups (475 ml) of water plus 2 tablespoons of desiccated coconut.

Reduce the heat to low and simmer, covered, until the chicken absorbs about half the marinade and is tender and cooked through, 45 minutes to 1 hour. Test the chicken for doneness by cutting into the meat near the bone. Stir occasionally so the chicken doesn't stick to the bottom of the pan.

Cool, then transfer the chicken and marinade to a container and marinate in the refrigerator for at least 8 hours. (Or freeze up to 1 month.)

Remove the chicken from the refrigerator at least 30 minutes before cooking. Prepare a paper towel–lined plate or a wire rack.

Heat about 2 inches (5 cm) oil in a wok or Dutch oven (4 qt/3.7 L) over high heat until an instant-read thermometer reads 375°F (190°C). (See page 200 for deep-frying tips.)

When the oil is hot, reduce the heat to medium. Use tongs to pick up the chicken pieces and shake off excess marinade. Fry the chicken pieces in batches, lowering them gently into the hot oil, until nicely browned, about 1 minute. The chicken is already cooked so all you're doing is browning the skin.

Drain on the paper towels or rack. Save the leftover marinade to make Tahu Tempe Bacem (see sidebar below). Bring the oil back up to temperature before frying the next batch.

Serve with steamed rice, Julia's Sambal Terasi (page 169), and a vegetable side dish like Sayur Asam (page 43) or Sambal Goreng Sayur Udang (page 100).

TAHU TEMPE BACEM

Instead of chicken, you can use 2 lb (1 kg) of tofu and/or tempeh cut into 3-inch (7.5-cm) squares or similarly sized triangles. Simmer until most of the liquid has evaporated and the flavors have been absorbed, about 45 minutes, flipping the tofu and tempeh halfway through cooking (when the liquid has reduced by about half).

You can also reuse the leftover marinade from making the chicken to marinate 1 lb (450 g) tofu and/or tempeh. The chicken has already been cooked so it's okay to reuse the marinade. To refresh, add 1 tablespoon of palm sugar, ½ teaspoon of salt, ½ teaspoon of ground coriander, and 1 salam leaf. Once deep-fried or pan-fried, tahu tempe bacem will be the most flavorful tofu or tempeh you've ever eaten.

Beef and Pork

In Indonesia, beef is not as often consumed as fish, seafood, and chicken. Since it is a relatively expensive ingredient, it's usually saved for special occasions to make dishes like Rendang Daging (page 67). Even though Muslims make up the majority of Indonesia's population, pork is eaten widely in Hindu Bali and by non-Muslims of Chinese descent. Babi Kecap (page 62) and Sate Babi Oma (page 139) are everyday dishes featuring pork that my family enjoys.

Indonesian-Style Beef Stew

SEMUR DAGING

*Makes 4 servings as part of
a multicourse meal*

FOR THE SPICE PASTE

6 Asian shallots or 3 European
shallots, chopped

4 medium-hot finger-length
red chilies, such as Fresno,
serrano, or cayenne, seeded
(optional) and chopped

3 cloves garlic, smashed

3 tablespoons vegetable
oil, divided

2 salam leaves or bay leaves

1 thumb-size piece fresh
ginger, smashed

2-inch (5-cm) cinnamon stick

1 lb (450 g) stew beef, such
as boneless chuck or
brisket, trimmed of excess
fat and gristle, cut into
1-inch (2.5-cm) cubes

3 cups (700 ml) water

½ cup (120 ml) kecap manis

2 tablespoons shaved palm
sugar or brown sugar

1½ teaspoons fine sea salt

½ teaspoon ground white
or black pepper

1 lb (450 g) yellow gold potatoes,
cut into 2-inch (5-cm) cubes

1 Roma tomato, chopped

Fried shallots for garnish

Oma says:

If there is too much sauce,
strain the meat and vegetables.
Then turn the heat to high
and reduce to your liking.
This way, the ingredients
don't get overcooked.

This dish has been around in the Indonesian culinary lexicon for a very long time but didn't always have a proper name. When the Dutch colonists arrived, they really liked the dish and dubbed it "smoor," which refers to a slow-cooking method. Over the years, the word *smoor* was transliterated to the Indonesian *semur*. Sweet and a little soupy, semur is quite unlike a Western stew.

Because it's an easy dish to prepare in large quantities, Julia often made semur using both chicken and beef to feed our growing family. While beef semur is most popular, the same technique can be used with meatballs, tofu, and/or vegetables like eggplant and long beans.

To make the spice paste, pulse the shallots, chilies, and garlic with 1 tablespoon of oil in a small food processor or blender until the texture of oatmeal, about 1 minute. Scrape down the sides of the bowl as necessary. Or use a mortar and pestle.

Heat the remaining 2 tablespoons of oil in a wok or large, heavy pot over medium heat until shimmering hot. Fry the spice paste, salam leaves, ginger, and cinnamon stick until fragrant, 2–3 minutes. Add the beef cubes and sear until browned on all sides.

Add the water, kecap manis, palm sugar, salt, and white pepper. Reduce the heat to medium-low and simmer, covered, for 1 hour. Add the potatoes and tomato and simmer until the beef and potatoes are tender, 15–20 minutes. The sauce will be soupy, not thick like a Western stew. You can reduce it further if desired. Taste and adjust the seasonings if desired. You should be able to taste the sweetness of the kecap manis.

Shower with fried shallots and serve with steamed rice and a vegetable side dish.

Kecap Manis–Braised Pork

BABI KECAP

Makes 6 servings as part of a multicourse meal

2 lb (1 kg) skinless, boneless pork belly and/or pork shoulder, cut into 1 × 2-inch (2.5 × 5-cm) pieces

½ cup (120 ml) kecap manis, divided

2 teaspoons ground white or black pepper

2 tablespoons vegetable oil

8 Asian shallots or 4 European shallots, sliced

4 cloves garlic, sliced

4 (¼-inch/6-mm) slices fresh ginger

2 teaspoons fine sea salt

1 teaspoon sugar

2½ cups (600 ml) water

1 lb (450 g) yellow gold potatoes, peeled and cut into 2-inch (5-cm) cubes

1 small yellow onion, sliced

Fried shallots for garnish

NOTES

You can add hard-cooked eggs at the same time you add the potatoes. Leftovers taste even better the next day.

Like many Indonesian dishes, babi kecap is a dish of many influences. At the crossroads of semur (page 61) and Chinese red-cooked pork, this pork belly dish uses kecap manis as a dominant flavoring, along with fresh ginger.

Marinate the pork with ¼ cup (60 ml) of kecap manis and the white pepper in a large mixing bowl for about 1 hour.

Heat the oil in a large pot over medium-high heat until shimmering hot. Add the shallots, garlic, and ginger and fry until fragrant and wilted, about 1 minute. Add the pork and stir and cook until no longer pink, about 3 minutes. Add the salt, sugar, water, and remaining ¼ cup (60 ml) of kecap manis. The liquid should reach about three-fourths of the way up the pork. Add more water if necessary. Bring to a boil.

Reduce the heat to medium and simmer, covered, for 30 minutes. Add the potatoes and cook until they can be easily pierced with a fork, 10–15 minutes. If you would like the pork to be even more tender and you have time, simmer for another 15–30 minutes before adding the potatoes. Taste and adjust the seasonings if desired.

When the pork and potatoes are ready, add the onion and remove from the heat. Shower with fried shallots and serve with steamed rice and a vegetable side dish.

Oma says:

Seek out pork belly pieces that are evenly streaked with creamy white fat and lean meat.

NOTES
Instead of a cinnamon stick, you can choose any of the following: 1 teaspoon of ground cinnamon, nutmeg, cumin, and/or a few whole cloves.

Javanese Beefsteak

BISTIK JAWA

Makes 4-6 servings as part of a multicourse meal

2 tablespoons kecap manis

1 teaspoon Worcestershire sauce or soy sauce

½ teaspoon fine sea salt

½ teaspoon ground white or black pepper

¼ teaspoon ground nutmeg

1 lb (450 g) thin (¼-inch/6-mm) beefsteaks, such as eye of round, top round, or sirloin

FOR THE SAUCE

2 tablespoons unsalted butter, divided

1 clove garlic, chopped

1 tablespoon all-purpose flour

½ cup (120 ml) whole or 2 percent milk

½ cup (120 ml) low-sodium beef or chicken stock or water

2 tablespoons kecap manis

1 tablespoon sugar (optional)

½ teaspoon ground white or black pepper

½ teaspoon ground nutmeg

Fried shallots for garnish

Bistik Jawa is a perfect example of the fusion of European and local cuisine. This is the only way my dad, Rudy, eats his steak: thin cuts of meat marinated in kecap manis and spices, doused in sauce, and served with carrots, green beans, and roasted potatoes. My dad also likes green peas in his sauce, but you can omit them if you want. Keep in mind that the marinade and sauce are quite sweet—it's the Javanese way!—so feel free to reduce the amount of sugar or kecap manis.

Rub the kecap manis, Worcestershire sauce, salt, white pepper, and nutmeg into the steaks. Marinate for at least 2 hours and up to 8 hours. Drain and reserve the marinade.

To make the sauce, melt 1 tablespoon of butter in a large, heavy skillet over medium-low heat. Add the garlic and cook until fragrant, about 15 seconds. Sprinkle in the flour and stir with a wooden spoon until light brown, 3-4 minutes. Whisk in the reserved marinade, milk, stock, and kecap manis, stirring constantly to prevent lumps from forming. Add the sugar (if using), white pepper, and nutmeg. Simmer for a few extra minutes if you'd like a thicker sauce. Taste and adjust the seasonings if desired. Mix in the fried shallots and set aside.

Melt the remaining 1 tablespoon of butter in a large, heavy skillet (I use a 10-inch/25-cm cast-iron pan) over high heat until sizzling hot. Using tongs, carefully place 2-3 steaks in the pan and sear on each side for 20-30 seconds. This goes very quickly so keep your eye on the steaks. Transfer to a plate and tent with foil to keep warm. Repeat with the remaining steaks.

Serve the steaks immediately, sauce drizzled on top or on the side. You may slice the steaks and serve as a communal meal (makan tengah) or individually with buttered carrots, green beans, and rice or crinkle fries.

Oma says:
To check if the pan is hot enough, touch the edge of a steak to the pan. If it sizzles, it's ready.

OPA SAUCE

Kecap manis is considered Indonesia's national condiment—a must-have both in the kitchen and on the table. It flavors the ubiquitous Nasi Goreng (and my sheet-pan version on page 106) and is added to popular dishes like Semur Daging (page 61). Kecap manis is also used as a dipping sauce for everything from Ikan Goreng (page 71) to emping (crackers made from the melinjo nut).

And my dad, Rudy, is its biggest fan. He loves to pour kecap manis over everything. Even his grandsons know of his love for this condiment. They call it Opa Sauce!

When I say everything, I mean *everything*. Having been raised on an exclusive diet of Indonesian and Chinese food, he's not a huge fan of any other type of cuisine. Dad's solution when he's forced to eat anything else? Squirt kecap manis on his grilled pork chop and stir puddles of the dark, viscous sauce into his spaghetti.

Dad's favorite brand is Bango. Like magic, the red-capped bottle with a turquoise label appears on the dining table at mealtimes. And for trips away from home, Julia decants the dark, syrupy liquid into a travel-size container, perfect for tucking away snugly in Dad's man bag.

I've always been curious about Dad's kecap manis obsession. I knew the answer lay somewhere in his childhood.

Dad was born in 1939, just before World War II, the second-oldest of nine siblings. He survived the hardships of the Japanese Occupation—his father (my opa) was interned, and his mother (my oma) struggled to feed the family, selling snacks and cakes at the market to make ends meet. But there were happy memories, too: catching betta fish in the rice fields, hitching rides on Dutch army trucks, and flying homemade kites with his brothers.

According to Dad, mealtimes were chaotic. My oma was always cooking for a crowd, so easy one-pot dishes like Babi Kecap (page 62), bak kut (pork ribs and salted vegetable soup), and gado gado Cirebon (vegetables and chicken with peanut sauce and curry) were the norm. He and his siblings had to fight for choice cuts. If you were slow, all you'd get to eat were the scraps. I'm also sure that if you had to cook for that many children every day, you'd give up on trying to make the food tasty. So that meals would be more palatable, Dad always reached for the bottle of kecap manis on the table.

Nowadays, Dad may forget that it's time to eat his lunch, but he won't forget to put kecap manis on it. Due to the natural process of aging, he has lost most of his sense of smell and taste. He probably can't tell salty from sweet, let alone umami. But there he goes, pouring kecap manis over everything on his plate at every meal.

Beef Rendang

RENDANG DAGING

Makes 6–8 servings as part of a multicourse meal

FOR THE SPICE PASTE

8 candlenuts or unsalted macadamias

1 tablespoon coriander seeds or ground coriander

10 Asian shallots or 5 European shallots, chopped

6–8 medium-hot finger-length red chilies, such as Fresno, cayenne, or serrano, seeded (optional) and chopped

6 whole cloves

5 cloves garlic, smashed

1 small yellow onion, chopped

6 tablespoons (90 ml) vegetable oil, divided

¼ cup (25 g) medium-hot chili powder, such as gochugaru or Kashmiri chili powder

1 tablespoon ground turmeric

5 makrut lime leaves

2 dried or fresh turmeric leaves (optional)

2-inch (5-cm) cinnamon stick

3 (½-inch/12-mm) slices galangal

2 stalks lemongrass, trimmed and bruised

2½–3 lb (1.1–1.4 kg) well-marbled boneless beef chuck roast or bottom round, cut into 2-inch (5-cm) cubes

1 can (13.5 fl oz/400ml) unsweetened coconut milk

2 tablespoons sugar

1 tablespoon + 1 teaspoon fine sea salt

Perhaps you've seen a rendang recipe that calls for four to five hours of cooking? It's no exaggeration. Beef in Indonesia is very tough, as is buffalo meat, the traditional protein used in the Minangkabau region of West Sumatra where rendang originates. Lucky for you, this version takes a little less time (even less if you use an electric pressure cooker).

You'll find as many recipes for rendang as you'll find cooks. Ingredients like oyster mushrooms, chicken, and banana blossoms are not uncommon. Julia's take on rendang is an amalgamation of her personal preferences and her long tenure in Singapore. The use of gochugaru (Korean red pepper powder) is one of these quirks. She adds it more for color than anything else. If you can't find it, you can recreate the moderate smoky heat with ancho chili or a 50/50 blend of cayenne and smoked paprika.

To make the spice paste, toast the candlenuts and coriander seeds separately in a small, dry skillet over medium heat until fragrant and browned, 5-6 minutes each. Crush the candlenuts with the flat part of a knife's blade. Grind the coriander into a coarse powder with a spice grinder or mortar and pestle. (If using ground coriander, just add it to the food processor in the next step.)

In a small food processor or blender, pulse the candlenuts, coriander, shallots, chilies, cloves, garlic, and onion with 2 tablespoons of oil until the texture of oatmeal, about 1 minute. Scrape down the sides of the bowl as necessary. Or use a mortar and pestle. (If using a mortar and pestle, grind the coriander first, then add the rest of the ingredients one by one with a pinch of salt.)

Heat the remaining 4 tablespoons (60 ml) of oil in a wok or large, heavy pot or Dutch oven over medium heat until shimmering hot. Add the spice paste followed by the chili powder and turmeric. Toss in the lime leaves, turmeric leaves (if using), cinnamon stick, galangal, and lemongrass and stir and cook until it is very fragrant and has turned a few shades darker (this indicates the shallots are caramelizing), 5-7 minutes. Reduce the heat if the paste is browning too fast; you don't want the paste to burn. Once the moisture has evaporated, the ingredients will separate from the oil. The paste is now ready for the next step.

Recipe continues

You can also cook rendang in an electric pressure cooker. After adding the coconut milk, Pressure cook for 35 minutes on high and release the steam naturally. There will be a lot of sauce. Cook on Sauté until the sauce reduces to your liking.

Once the rendang has cooled to room temperature, store in an airtight container in the refrigerator for about 5 days. For longer storage, freezing is great as the braising liquid creates an airtight seal around the ingredients, protecting them from freezer burn. However, curries and heavily spiced dishes should not be kept in the freezer for long (about 1 month is good), as the flavors change and become more potent over time.

Add the beef and stir to coat with the spice paste. Stir and cook for 2–3 minutes. Add the coconut milk, sugar, and salt. Bring to a gentle boil, then reduce the heat to medium-low and simmer gently, uncovered, for about 2 hours. Keep stirring every 20 minutes or so to prevent the meat from sticking to the bottom of the pan. (Alternatively, transfer the beef mixture to a large baking dish and bake in a 250°F/120°C oven for 2 hours.)

After about 2 hours, the oil from the coconut milk will separate and rise to the surface, forming a slight sheen or a puddle of oil, depending on the fat content of the coconut milk. Only the meat, oils, and a thick sauce remain in the pot. At this stage, the dish is known as kalio and can be eaten as is. This is how Julia usually prepares rendang.

For a more traditional rendang, continue cooking until all the liquid evaporates. Reduce the heat to low and allow the beef to brown in the rendered fat until it caramelizes and darkens into the color of roasted coffee beans. Stir continuously for about 30 minutes longer. (See sidebar below.)

Once the beef is soft and tender enough to poke with a fork and the sauce is reduced to your liking, taste and adjust the seasonings if desired.

Fish out the whole herbs and spices and serve with steamed rice, Sambal Cabe Hijau (page 171), and a vegetable side dish. Or allow the flavors to meld for up to 2 hours at room temperature.

ABOUT RENDANG

The word *rendang* comes from a cooking method called merendang. It is the process of slow-cooking protein in coconut milk and spices to the point of caramelization, an essential technique that preserves meats for long periods of time in Indonesia's hot tropical climate.

There are three stages to cooking rendang. After an hour of simmering, when the ingredients are fully cooked and the coconut milk is boiling, the dish has reached the gulai stage. Gulai, or kare, is a stew not unlike the curries from other Southeast Asian neighbors. The resulting dish is still brothy and tinged a light yellow from the turmeric. At about the 2-hour mark, the second stage known as kalio is reached. The meat is cooked longer than gulai but only two-thirds of the way to rendang. At this stage, the oil splits from the coconut milk and forms puddles of oil on the surface of the thick, dark reddish-brown gravy. At this point, the sauce should be reduced by at least 60 percent.

The final stage is a somewhat dry dish that has been cooked until most of the coconut milk has evaporated. The small amount of liquid left appears very oily from the fat left behind and is a very dark espresso brown but not burned. This is the most traditional version of rendang. Some say the drier the rendang, the longer it keeps without refrigeration—sometimes up to months!

Today, the three dishes aren't usually labeled separately. More often, you will find either wet rendang (usually kalio) or dry rendang.

Fish and Seafood

Indonesia is an archipelago, so it's not surprising that fish and seafood are a huge part of our diet. We like our fish whole, complete with head and tail. Please do not fear. You can always have the fishmonger clean and gut your fish. Cooking fish on the bone is easy, and a whole fish has more flavor and stays juicier and moister than the usual fillets and steaks, no matter how they're prepared. Feel free to mix and match spice pastes, seasonings and cooking methods.

I'm used to eating shrimp with the head, shell, and tail on. However, I do understand not everyone enjoys them this way. You can use headless, peeled shrimp for all our recipes. However, buying intact shrimp allows you to make stock and results in juicier shrimp.

Squid used to be a specialty item but is now available at most supermarkets. I encourage you to try Cumi Lada Hitam (page 79). Above all, please buy the best-quality fish and seafood you can afford and try to source sustainably.

Simple Fried Fish

IKAN GORENG

Makes 2–3 servings as part of a multicourse meal

1 (1-lb/450-g) whole firm, white-fleshed fish, such Spanish mackerel or white bass, scaled, cleaned, and gutted

Juice of 1 key lime

1 teaspoon fine sea salt or a flaky, fancy salt like Himalayan pink salt

Vegetable oil for frying

NOTES

Your fishmonger will scale and gut your fish for you. At H Mart and many other Asian markets, the prep styles are numbered from 1–6. Choose from butterfly cut, fish steaks, fillet, gut and head off, scale, and gut. Some markets even offer deep-frying services. If you prefer, buy 1-inch (2.5-cm) fish steaks and fry for about 6 minutes total, flipping halfway through cooking.

For more complex flavor, you can rub the fish with ground turmeric and/or coriander, tamarind, or a spice paste.

Oma says:

"Wash" the fish with lime juice "supaya nggak amis" so that it doesn't smell fishy.

I struggle with cooking fish at home, and most of the time, it's boring salmon fillets or fish sticks. I miss the wide array of fish and cooking methods I grew up with. Julia would often deep-fry mackerel (tenggiri) or threadfin (kurau) for a simple meal served with Sambal Kecap (page 166) and a side of stir-fried spinach. As a child, it wasn't my favorite meal. However, I can now appreciate that it's speedy and fuss-free.

Unlike the battered fried fish common in the United States, whole fish or fish steaks are preferred in Indonesia. This method is not suitable for fillets. That being said, neutral-flavored, white-fleshed, and lean fish are best for frying. Freshwater fish such as mackerel, tilapia, striped or white bass, trout, and perch are excellent choices.

Use a sharp paring knife to make 3–4 deep cuts at an angle toward the head (this is called scoring), about 1 inch (2.5 cm) apart on both sides of the fish.

Squeeze the lime juice over both sides of the fish and set aside for 10 minutes. Pat dry with paper towels, then rub the salt into both sides of the fish and inside the score lines and the belly cavity.

Refrigerate, uncovered, for 30 minutes to 1 hour to dry out.

When ready to fry, pat the fish as dry as possible with paper towels. This prevents splattering when the fish enters the hot oil.

Heat about 1 inch (2.5 cm) of oil in a wok or large, heavy skillet over high heat until shimmering hot. Reduce the heat to medium and carefully lower the fish into the hot oil. The oil should reach about halfway up the fish. (If you prefer to deep-fry, you can. See page 200 for tips.)

Fry the fish until crispy and golden on both sides, 12–15 minutes, flipping carefully halfway through cooking with rubber tongs or a flat spatula.

Serve the fish with steamed rice, a vegetable side dish, and your favorite sambal, or Sweet and Sour Sauce (page 91).

Shrimp Cooked in Oyster Sauce

UDANG MASAK SAUS TIRAM

Makes 4 servings as part of a multicourse meal

1 lb (450 g) jumbo (26/30) raw tail-on shrimp, peeled and deveined

1 teaspoon fine sea salt

½ teaspoon ground white or black pepper

¼ cup (60 ml) vegetable oil, plus more as needed

5 cloves garlic, minced

1 small yellow onion, sliced

2 medium-hot finger-length chilies, such as Fresno, serrano, or cayenne, seeded (optional) and sliced, or 1 tablespoon sambal oelek (optional)

1 small green or red bell pepper, sliced

3 tablespoons oyster sauce

2 tablespoons kecap manis

1 tablespoon soy sauce

¼ cup (60 ml) + 1 tablespoon water, divided

½ teaspoon cornstarch

NOTES

Don't be put off by frozen shrimp. The shelf life of thawed shrimp is only a couple of days, but shrimp stored in the freezer retain their quality for several weeks.

This is an easy and delicious weeknight meal with rice and a vegetable side dish. I'd cook it more often, if only my son liked shrimp! Frozen shrimp usually has salt added, so you may want to reduce the amount of salt to ½ teaspoon.

Toss the shrimp with the salt and white pepper in a medium bowl and marinate for 15 minutes. Pat dry with paper towels so the shrimp don't splatter when entering the oil.

Heat the oil in a wok or large, heavy skillet over medium-high heat until shimmering hot. Add the shrimp and stir and cook until they just turn pink, 1–2 minutes. Transfer to a plate lined with paper towels.

If there are less than 2 tablespoons of oil left in the wok, top it up and heat over medium heat until shimmering hot. Add the garlic and onion and stir and cook until fragrant, about 1 minute. Add the chilies (if using) and bell pepper, followed by the oyster sauce, kecap manis, soy sauce, and ¼ cup (60 ml) of water. Cook until the bell pepper is tender-crisp, about 2 minutes, or cooked to your liking. Taste and adjust the seasonings if desired.

In a small bowl, combine the remaining 1 tablespoon of water and the cornstarch to create a slurry. Add the slurry and cooked shrimp to the wok and stir and cook until the sauce is thickened and the shrimp are heated through.

Serve with steamed rice and a vegetable dish.

Roasted Whole Fish Rubbed with Spice Paste

IKAN BAKAR

Makes 4 servings as part of a multicourse meal

1 (1–1½ lb/450–680 g) whole fish, such as red snapper, branzino, or porgy, scaled, cleaned, and gutted

Juice of 1 key lime

1½ teaspoons fine sea salt, divided

1 teaspoon coriander seeds or ground coriander

4 Asian shallots or 2 European shallots, chopped

2 cloves garlic, smashed

½ oz (15 g) fresh ginger, chopped

2 teaspoons ground turmeric

2 tablespoons vegetable oil, divided

¼ teaspoon ground white or black pepper

2 tablespoons kecap manis

Cooking spray for greasing

When in Indonesia, we would always have ikan bakar, whole fish grilled over a charcoal fire. However, I'm always looking for easier and faster ways to serve my family fish, so I roast it in the oven. The first time I served whole fish to my husband and son, they spent the entire meal complaining about having to pick out bones. If that's the case in your family, too, I feel your pain and give you full permission to resort to fish fillets. But please know that having whole fish is such a treat! The flesh is so much more succulent and flavorful, and nothing is wasted because you can gnaw on the cheeks and crunch on the fins and tail. Thankfully, your fishmonger can gut and scale your fish, so that unpleasant job is taken care of.

Use a sharp paring knife to make 3–4 deep cuts at an angle toward the head (this is called scoring), about 1 inch (2.5 cm) apart on both sides of the fish.

Squeeze the lime juice and sprinkle 1 teaspoon of salt on both sides of the fish. Set aside while you make the spice paste.

To make the spice paste, toast the coriander seeds in a small, dry skillet over medium heat until fragrant and browned, 5–6 minutes. Grind into a coarse powder with a spice grinder or mortar and pestle. (If using ground coriander, just add it to the food processor in the next step.)

In a small food processor or blender, pulse the coriander, shallots, garlic, ginger, and turmeric with 1 tablespoon of oil until the texture of oatmeal, about 1 minute. Scrape down the sides of the bowl as necessary. Or use a mortar and pestle. (If using a mortar and pestle, grind the coriander first, then add the rest of the ingredients one by one with a pinch of salt.)

Heat the remaining 1 tablespoon of oil in a small skillet over medium heat until shimmering hot. Fry the spice paste until fragrant, about 2 minutes. Add the remaining ½ teaspoon of salt and the white pepper and stir and cook until the oil separates from the paste and the paste has turned a few shades darker (this indicates the shallots are caramelizing), another 2–3 minutes. Reduce the heat if the paste is browning too fast; you don't want the paste to burn. Remove from the heat. Add the kecap manis and stir to mix.

Recipe continues

To grill, place the fish in a fish basket and grill over medium heat (450°F/230°C on a gas grill) until an instant-read thermometer inserted into the thickest part registers 135°F (57°C), 15–20 minutes.

Line a rimmed baking sheet with aluminum foil and spray with cooking spray. Spread the spice paste on both sides of the fish, making sure to go inside the cuts and the belly. Save about 2 tablespoons for basting. Place the fish on the baking sheet, cover, and refrigerate for at least 30 minutes.

Preheat the oven to 400°F (200°C).

Roast the fish for 15–20 minutes, until an instant-read thermometer inserted into the thickest part registers 135°F (57°C). Halfway through the cooking time, brush one side of the fish with the reserved spice paste, flip, and brush the other side.

Let the fish rest for 5 minutes, then transfer to a serving platter. Serve with Sambal Kecap (page 166), steamed rice, and a vegetable side like Lalapan (page 94), Sambal Kangkung (page 98), or Sayur Asam (page 43). Use a spoon and a fork to lift the meat off the bones and distribute among diners.

FROM OUR RECIPE TESTERS
"I was really nervous about cooking a whole fish—it was my first time," says recipe tester Marcie Flinchum Atkins. "I've only had it out at restaurants in Thailand. It was easy, and the flavor was great!"

Julia's Chili Crab

KEPITING SAUS JULIA

Makes 4 servings as part of a multicourse meal

2 tablespoons vegetable oil

3 cloves garlic, minced

3 Asian shallots or 1 European shallot, chopped

½ oz (15 g) fresh ginger, peeled and minced

2 cups (475 ml) homemade or store-bought low-sodium chicken broth

1 cup (225 g) all-natural or organic tomato ketchup

2 tablespoons sambal oelek

1 tablespoon sherry or vermouth (optional)

2 teaspoons sugar

1½ teaspoons fine sea salt

2 lb (1 kg) Dungeness or snow crab legs (3–4 clusters), thawed if frozen, split into 2- or 3-leg sections, and shells cracked with a meat pounder or nutcracker

2 large eggs, beaten

2 teaspoons cornstarch or tapioca flour

2 tablespoons water

¼ cup (23 g) thinly sliced green onions (optional)

¼ cup (7 g) fresh cilantro leaves (optional)

Steamed rice, man tou, or crusty bread for serving

My extended family has made serving chili crab at Thanksgiving a tradition. Julia's recipe is a cross between Singapore chili crab and Indonesian-style kepiting saus Padang (crab cooked Padang-style, i.e., very spicy!). She would usually buy live crabs from the market and kill them just before cooking. I did this once and prefer not to repeat the experience, so I'm using crab leg clusters instead. I'm only using 2 lb (1 kg) of crab legs because we usually have this dish together with a host of other sides. In addition, not all of us enjoy the task of breaking the shell and picking out the crab meat. I, for one, prefer to eat just the sauce with man tou (Chinese buns). Feel free to buy more crab if you are feeding crab lovers (usually 1 lb/450 g per person) and multiply the other ingredients accordingly.

Heat the oil in a large wok or Dutch oven over medium heat until shimmering hot. Add the garlic, shallots, and ginger and fry until fragrant, 30 seconds to 1 minute.

Add the broth, ketchup, sambal, and sherry (if using). Stir to mix, then add the sugar and salt. You may want to adjust depending on how sweet or salty your ketchup is. Simmer until the sauce starts to bubble gently, 1–2 minutes. The sauce should be a nice balance of sweet, salt, and spice.

Add the crab legs, bending and tucking them as needed to fit in the wok. Stir and coat the crab with the sauce. Cover and simmer until the crab is heated through and has absorbed some of the sauce, 5–6 minutes. Be careful not to overcook as the crab meat will toughen and lose its delicate flavor. Transfer the crab to a serving platter.

Raise the heat to medium-high. Swirl the beaten eggs into the sauce in a thin, circular stream. Once the egg is barely set, 45 seconds to 1 minute, give the sauce a quick stir. There should be no lumps.

In a small bowl, combine the cornstarch and water to create a slurry. Add the slurry and stir until the sauce thickens, 1–2 minutes.

Pour the sauce over the cooked crab. Sprinkle with the green onions and cilantro (if using) and serve immediately with rice. Have mallets, nutcrackers, and/or kitchen shears available for splitting. To eat, pour the sauce over rice and eat with crab meat, or dip crab meat and/or pieces of bread into the sauce.

NOTES

If buying whole squid, look for specimens weighing less than 10 oz (285 g) each. They're more tender when cooked. You can buy whole squid from the seafood counter. It may or may not be cleaned, but don't be shy to ask the fishmonger to do it for you. I buy it frozen from the freezer section, which is probably flash frozen and already cleaned.

For this recipe, it's best to start with whole black peppercorns and coriander seeds and grind them coarsely, preferably with a mortar and pestle.

Black Pepper Squid

CUMI LADA HITAM

Makes 4 servings as part of a multicourse meal

1 lb (450 g) squid tubes and tentacles, cleaned

2 teaspoons baking soda

2 tablespoons kecap manis

2 tablespoons oyster sauce

2 tablespoons sugar

2 tablespoons water

½ cup (70 g) rice flour

2 tablespoons cornstarch

½ teaspoon fine sea salt

¼ teaspoon ground white or black pepper

Vegetable oil for frying

2 teaspoons unsalted butter

3 cloves garlic, finely chopped

2 teaspoons grated fresh ginger

1 medium-hot finger-length red chili, such as Fresno, cayenne, or serrano, seeded (optional) and very finely chopped, or 2 teaspoons sambal oelek (optional)

1 tablespoon black peppercorns, coarsely ground

¼ teaspoon coriander seeds, coarsely ground

2 green onions, finely chopped

2 tablespoons chopped cilantro leaves

You may have heard of fried calamari? Well, cumi (pronounced "choo-me"), squid, and calamari are just different names for the cephalopod related to both the cuttlefish and the octopus. For tender, tasty squid, cook it either hot and fast (deep-fry or grill for no more than 2 minutes) or poach it for at least 30 minutes. Anything in between gives rubbery results. This dish, with a sauce similar to Singapore's popular black pepper crab, fits into the former category. Feel free to try the sauce with tofu, chicken, or shrimp!

Cut the squid tubes into ½-inch (12-mm) rings. Place the squid in a medium bowl with enough water to cover by 1 inch (2.5 cm), then stir in the baking soda. Leave at room temperature for 30 minutes. Rinse several times with water and drain in a colander. Pat the squid as dry as possible with paper towels. This will help the squid crisp up when fried.

In a small bowl, stir together the kecap manis, oyster sauce, sugar, and water. Set aside.

Mix together the rice flour, cornstarch, salt, and white pepper in a large bowl. Dredge half the squid pieces in the flour mixture so they are evenly coated and place in a dry colander. Repeat with the rest of the squid.

Heat 2 inches (5 cm) of oil in a small pot (I use about 4 cups/950 ml oil in a 2.5-quart/2.3-L pot) over high heat until an instant-read thermometer reads 350°F (180°C). (See page 200 for deep-frying tips.)

Use tongs to pick up squid pieces one at a time and shake off excess flour. Lower into the hot oil, making sure they float freely and don't touch the bottom of the pan. Fry in batches until crispy, 1½–2 minutes. Drain on paper towels or a wire rack and, if possible, keep warm in a 250°F (120°C) oven. Bring the oil back up to temperature before frying the next batch. Repeat until all the squid is fried.

Melt the butter with 2 teaspoons of oil in a large skillet over medium heat. Fry the garlic, ginger, chilies (if using), black pepper, and coriander until fragrant, 30 seconds to 1 minute. Stir in the kecap manis mixture and simmer until thick and sticky, about 1 minute. Toss the cooked squid in the sauce and stir until well coated and warmed through, about 1 minute. Add the green onions and give everything a quick stir. Transfer to a serving plate, sprinkle with cilantro, and serve with steamed rice and a vegetable side dish.

Eggs, Tofu, and Tempeh

In a country where meat isn't always affordable, eggs, tofu, and tempeh provide valuable protein and form a very important part of the Indonesian diet. It's not unusual to have two or three dishes based on these ingredients for an entire meal. One of my favorite tofu and tempeh preparations, Tahu Tempe Bacem (page 59), mimics the chicken dish Ayam Goreng Manis (page 58).

Eggs are a welcome by-product of the scrawny chickens (ayam kampung) that ply rural villages and can be prepared in the simplest of ways. Case in point: my dad's favorite, Ceplok Telur (page 81), is a sunny-side up egg with frilly golden edges served on a bed of rice and topped with a drizzle of kecap manis and fried shallots. We also eat hearty omelets filled with shrimp and vegetables (Foo Yong Hai, page 91) or tofu (Tahu Telur, page 88), and eggs scrambled with vegetables (Orak Arik Buncis Wortel, page 82).

Tofu and tempeh are both soy products; tofu is made from soy milk and tempeh, from the whole bean. While tofu is a Chinese import, tempeh is a traditional superfood, first recorded sometime in the eighteenth century. I must admit that I shunned tofu and tempeh when I was a child (except for Tempe Orek Kering page 84). However, I have seen the light. Now, I tell anyone who says that tofu and tempeh are bland that they must try them prepared the Indonesian way. The truth is, tofu and tempeh are blank canvases that soak up flavors beautifully. When fried, stir-fried, or tossed into spiced braises, they come out nutritious and delicious.

Fried Egg

CEPLOK TELUR

Makes 1 serving

1 tablespoon vegetable oil

1 large egg

Steamed rice for serving

Kecap manis for serving

Fried shallots for serving

Ceplok telur is an egg fried sunny-side up. This way of cooking an egg is also called "telor mata sapi" or "eye of the cow egg." A plate of rice topped off with ceplok telur, drizzled with kecap manis, and showered with fried shallots makes the perfect lazy meal. You can, of course, make the yolk as runny or as firm as you'd like!

Heat the oil in a small cast-iron or nonstick skillet over medium-high heat until shimmering hot. Carefully break the egg close to the surface of the oil to prevent hot oil from splashing.

Tilt the skillet toward you so oil pools against the side of the pan. Baste the egg with the hot oil, aiming at the uncooked portions of the egg white and avoiding the yolk. Continue basting until the egg is puffy and cooked and the edges are ruffled and brown, 45 seconds to 1 minute. (Flip if you prefer your fried egg over easy or well-done.) Transfer to a plate.

Repeat as many times as desired, but be sure to add more oil and pause to get it nice and hot again.

Serve over steamed rice, drizzled with kecap manis and sprinkled with fried shallots.

FROM OUR RECIPE TESTERS
If frying more than one egg, recipe tester Naomi Capili suggests breaking all the eggs into a bowl, then pouring 1 egg at a time close to the pan surface. "It keeps your fingers from getting dirty each time you crack a new egg, and the cooking flow is nice and easy," she says.

Eggy Stir-Fry with Green Beans and Carrots

ORAK ARIK TELUR BUNCIS WORTEL

Makes 4 servings as part of a multicourse meal

2 tablespoons vegetable oil

4 Asian shallots or 2 European shallots, minced

4 cloves garlic, minced

1 teaspoon ground turmeric (optional)

½ lb (225 g) carrots, cut into matchsticks

½ lb (225 g) green beans, cut into 2-inch (5-cm) pieces

4 large eggs, lightly beaten

1½ teaspoons fine sea salt

1 teaspoon sugar

½ teaspoon ground white or black pepper

2 green onions, green parts only, chopped

Handful Chinese celery leaves or parsley for garnish

The term *orak arik* literally means "to scramble." You can orak arik pretty much anything with eggs. Quick and easy to make, this recipe was a lifesaver for Julia when she was a busy mother of three young'uns. Use any vegetable you like—cabbage, chayote, spinach—anything goes! In summer, I like zucchini in lieu of the green beans. Vegan? Use tofu instead of eggs. Have a meat lover in the house? Add some ground meat. The possibilities are endless!

Heat the oil in a wok or large, heavy skillet over medium-high heat until shimmering hot. Add the shallots and garlic and stir and cook until fragrant, 1–2 minutes. Add the turmeric (if using) and stir and cook until it releases its aroma and darkens, about 1 minute.

Add the carrots and green beans and toss to coat. Stir and cook until soft, 2–3 minutes.

Pour the beaten eggs over the vegetables and cook undisturbed until the eggs start to set, about 1 minute. Break up the egg into large curds and mix into the vegetables.

Season with the salt, sugar, and white pepper and stir and cook until the vegetables are cooked to your liking. I like my carrots a little firm. Stir in the green onions. Taste and adjust the seasonings if desired.

Transfer to a serving bowl and shower with celery leaves. Serve with steamed rice and a meat dish.

Fried Tofu and Tempeh

TAHU TEMPE GORENG

Makes 4 servings as part of a multicourse meal

½ lb (225 g) firm or extra-firm tofu, drained

½ lb (225 g) tempeh

3 cloves garlic

1½ teaspoons salt, or to taste

1 teaspoon coriander seeds or ground coriander

½ cup (120 ml) water

Vegetable oil for frying

NOTES
Fried tofu and tempeh can be made ahead and stored in a sealed container in the fridge.

Toss tofu and tempeh pieces in 1–2 tablespoons of oil. Roast in a convection oven at 450°F (230°C) for 20–25 minutes, turning halfway through cooking, until golden brown on both sides. Or air-fry for 12–15 minutes.

Oma says:
Better a saltier marinade than a bland one. In the process of frying, the salt will leach out into the oil.

Tofu and tempeh are often paired together, and the simplest way to prepare them is to deep-fry. Fried tofu or tempeh is eaten with steamed rice, sambal, and Lalapan (page 94) for a simple yet complete meal. Or add bite-size pieces to vegetable dishes to pump up the protein. Before you start cooking, read page 200 for deep-frying tips.

Cut the tofu and tempeh into slabs ¼–½ inch (6–12 mm) thick or your choice of shape and size. (If making bite-size pieces to add to other dishes, cut into 1-inch/2.5-cm cubes.)

Grind the garlic, salt, and coriander with a mortar and pestle until a rough paste forms. Add the water to the mortar and stir until the salt dissolves. Taste. The marinade should be salty as the flavor will dissipate when fried in oil. Add more salt if desired. If the mortar is small, transfer the marinade to a large bowl.

Soak both sides of the tofu and tempeh pieces in the marinade for at least 15 minutes and up to 1 hour. Remove from the marinade and pat dry with paper towels to prevent splattering when frying.

Heat about 1 inch (2.5 cm) of oil in a wok or large, heavy skillet over high heat until shimmering hot. Use tongs to carefully dip the edge of a tempeh piece into the oil. If bubbles gather around it, the oil is hot enough.

Gently slide in as many pieces of tofu and tempeh as will fit in your pan without touching and fry, turning occasionally, until golden and crispy, 3–5 minutes. Don't cook them for too long or they will turn dry and hard.

Remove with tongs or a wire-mesh strainer and drain on a wire rack or paper towels. Bring the oil temperature back up to 350°F (180°C) before cooking the next batch. Repeat until all the tofu and tempeh is cooked.

Serve the fried tempeh and tofu with steamed rice, Julia's Sambal Terasi (page 169), and Lalapan (page 94).

Tamarind-Glazed Baked Tempeh

TEMPE OREK KERING

*Makes 2 servings as part of
a multicourse meal*

1 package (½ lb/225 g) tempeh,
cut into small rectangles
or matchsticks

5 tablespoons (75 ml)
vegetable oil, divided

2 small Asian shallots or 1 large
European shallot, sliced

2 cloves garlic, sliced

3 (½-inch/12-mm)
slices galangal

2 makrut lime leaves, crushed

1 stalk lemongrass,
trimmed and bruised

2 teaspoons sambal
oelek, or to taste

¼ cup (60 ml) Air Asam (page
188) or ½ cup (120 ml) store-
bought tamarind concentrate

3 tablespoons shaved palm
sugar or brown sugar

¼ teaspoon fine sea salt

1 tablespoon water, plus
more as needed

NOTES
Preheat an air fryer to 400°F
(200°C). Place the oil-covered
tempeh in a single layer in your
air fryer basket or tray and cook
for 15–20 minutes, or until the
tempeh is firm, crispy, and golden.

This dish of crispy tempeh bits doused in a sweet and sour tamarind sauce disguises the true funky taste of tempeh. It's a great introductory dish for anyone new to tempeh. Julia deep-fries her tempeh, but I prefer to bake it in the oven until crisp. If you can't find all the herbs, just gather as many as you can. The dish will still be tasty. The recipe is easily scaled up to feed more people.

Preheat the oven to 400°F (200°C) on the convection setting or to 425°F (220°C) on the standard bake setting. Line a baking sheet with aluminum foil.

Toss the tempeh with 2 tablespoons of oil. Spread on the prepared baking sheet in a single layer. Roast for 20 minutes, until golden brown. If not using the convection setting, flip the tempeh halfway through the cooking time. Set aside.

Heat the remaining 3 tablespoons of oil in a large skillet over medium heat until shimmering hot. Stir and cook the shallots and garlic until fragrant, about 30 seconds. Add the galangal, lime leaves, lemongrass, and sambal and give everything a quick stir until aromatic, about 30 seconds.

Add the air asam, palm sugar, salt, and water. Cook, stirring, until the sugar melts and a sticky sauce forms, 2–4 minutes.

Add the tempeh and stir and cook until well coated, adding water, 1 tablespoon at a time, if necessary. Taste and adjust the seasonings if desired. You want a combination of sweet, spicy, and sour flavors.

Fish out the large herbs and serve immediately with steamed rice and a vegetable side dish.

Tofu Cutlets

PERKEDEL TAHU

*Makes 4 servings as part of
a multicourse meal or 6 servings
as an appetizer*

1 package (1 lb/450 g)
 medium-firm tofu

¼ lb (115 g) ground beef,
 pork, or chicken

¼ lb (115 g) peeled and
 chopped raw shrimp

6 Asian shallots or
 3 European shallots

3 cloves garlic, smashed

½ teaspoon fine sea salt

½ teaspoon ground white
 or black pepper

¼ teaspoon sugar

1 teaspoon vegetable oil,
 plus more for frying

2 large eggs, beaten

3 tablespoons all-purpose flour

2 green onions, finely chopped

These delicious cutlets are satisfying both as part of a meal or as a snack. My son and husband can devour three or four at a time! Note that these cutlets are not vegetarian. You can adjust the amount of meat and shrimp as desired or omit them completely.

Wrap the tofu in a non-terry kitchen towel and wring out as much liquid as possible. You will have about 2 cups (450 g) of crumbled tofu. Mix the crumbled tofu with the ground beef and shrimp in a large bowl.

To make the spice paste, pulse the shallots, garlic, salt, white pepper, and sugar with 1 teaspoon of oil in a small food processor or blender until the texture of oatmeal, about 1 minute. Or use a mortar and pestle.

Add the beaten eggs and flour to the tofu mixture and mix well until well incorporated. Add the spice paste and green onions to the tofu-meat mixture.

Divide the mixture into 12 balls and flatten into disks 2–3 inches (5–7.5 cm) in diameter.

Heat ½–1 inch (12 mm–2.5 cm) of oil in a wok or large, heavy saucepan over high heat until shimmering hot. Reduce the heat to medium and fry the cutlets in batches, making sure they don't touch each other. They will not be submerged in oil. Bathe the cutlets with oil and fry until golden brown on both sides and cooked through, 5–6 minutes, flipping halfway through cooking. Drain on paper towels or a wire rack.

Serve with steamed rice and a vegetable side like Cap Cay (page 93).

Tofu Omelet

TAHU TELUR

Makes 4 servings as part of a multicourse meal

FOR THE SAUCE

1 tablespoon dried shrimp (optional)

¼ cup (70 g) smooth peanut butter

3 tablespoons kecap manis

¼ cup (60 ml) hot water

2 teaspoons sambal oelek

1 teaspoon distilled white vinegar

¼ teaspoon fine sea salt

5 large eggs

1 teaspoon cornstarch

½ teaspoon fine sea salt

¼ teaspoon ground white or black pepper

1 package (14 oz/400 g) firm tofu, drained and cut into ½-inch (12-mm) cubes

Vegetable oil for frying

1 cup (90 g) bean sprouts, blanched, or 1 small Persian cucumber, cut into strips

Chopped Chinese celery leaves or parsley for serving

Fried shallots for serving

Fried garlic for serving (optional)

This dish wasn't always in Julia's repertoire. When we lived in Singapore, we used to dine at an Indonesian restaurant called Sanur. We didn't eat there often but when we did, we always ordered tahu telur, a crispy nest of tofu and eggs fried together into an elevated omelet and drizzled with a heady sweet and spicy sauce. My siblings and I convinced Julia to recreate this dish at home so that we could eat it all the time. While it isn't as spectacular in presentation, it is just as tasty.

To make the sauce, toast the dried shrimp (if using) in a small, dry skillet until fragrant, about 1 minute. When cool enough to handle, grind into a coarse powder with a mortar and pestle or mince it. Stir together the toasted dried shrimp, peanut butter, kecap manis, and water in a medium bowl. Whisk into a smooth paste. Stir in the sambal, vinegar, and salt. Taste and adjust the seasonings if desired.

Beat together the eggs, cornstarch, salt, and white pepper in a large bowl. Gently fold in the tofu.

Heat ½ inch (12 mm) of oil in a large nonstick skillet or 10-inch (25-cm) cast-iron pan over medium-high heat until shimmering hot. Pour in the tofu-egg mixture and spread the tofu out as evenly as possible, shaking and swirling the pan so the egg spreads out, too.

Cook until the underside is golden brown and the edges start to crisp up, 5–6 minutes. Flip the omelet, adding a little more oil to the pan if it looks dry, and cook until the egg is set and both sides are golden brown, 2–3 minutes longer. Slide the omelet onto a large serving plate. Try to keep it in one piece, but if it breaks up, don't worry about it.

Pour the sauce over the omelet and garnish with bean sprouts, celery leaves, fried shallots, and fried garlic (if using). Serve with Lontong (page 182) if desired.

Vegetable and Shrimp Omelet with Sweet and Sour Sauce

FOO YONG HAI

Makes 4 servings as part of a multicourse meal

3 tablespoons vegetable oil, divided

2 cups (170 g) finely shredded cabbage

1 carrot, peeled and cut into matchsticks

¾ teaspoon fine sea salt, divided

6 large eggs

1 teaspoon cornstarch

¼ teaspoon ground white or black pepper

1 green onion, chopped

3 oz (90 g) raw peeled shrimp, finely chopped (optional)

FOR THE SWEET AND SOUR SAUCE

1 teaspoon vegetable oil

2 cloves garlic, minced

½ cup (120 ml) + 2 tablespoons water, divided

¼ cup (60 g) organic or all-natural ketchup

2 tablespoons rice vinegar

2–3 teaspoons sugar

1 teaspoon fine sea salt

2 tablespoons chopped yellow onion (optional)

¼ cup (35 g) frozen green peas, thawed (optional)

2 teaspoons cornstarch

Oma says:
For even easier prep, buy packaged coleslaw mix from the store.

A staple on our dinner table when I was growing up, foo yong hai is a Chinese-influenced dish. You may find a similar dish at Chinese-American restaurants doused in brown gravy called egg foo young. I may be biased, but Julia's version is tastier!

Heat 1 tablespoon of oil in a wok or 10-inch (25-cm) cast-iron or nonstick skillet over medium-high heat until shimmering hot. Add the cabbage, carrot, and ¼ teaspoon of salt. Stir and cook until wilted, 2–3 minutes. Remove from the heat and allow to cool while you beat the eggs.

Beat the eggs with the cornstarch in a large bowl until frothy. Season with the remaining ½ teaspoon of salt and the white pepper. Fold in the cooked cabbage and carrot, green onion, and shrimp (if using).

Using the same pan, heat 1 tablespoon of oil over medium-high heat until shimmering hot. Reduce the heat to medium. Pour half the egg mixture into the pan. Cook until the bottom is golden brown (lift up the edge to take a peek) and the top is drying up, 2–3 minutes. Flip carefully and cook the other side until the egg is cooked through and both sides are golden brown, 1–1½ minutes longer. Slide the omelet onto a plate.

Using the same pan, heat the remaining 1 tablespoon of oil and repeat with the rest of the egg mixture.

To make the sauce, heat the oil in a saucepan over medium heat until shimmering hot. Add the garlic and stir until fragrant, about 45 seconds. Add ½ cup (120 ml) of water, the ketchup, vinegar, sugar, and salt. Whisk until smooth. Taste and adjust the seasonings. The sauce should taste sweet and sour, but the flavor balance will depend on the ketchup you use. Add the onion and peas (if using) and simmer until the onion is translucent but still crunchy, 2–3 minutes.

In a small bowl, stir together the remaining 2 tablespoons of water and the cornstarch to make a slurry. Pour the slurry into the saucepan and bring to a gentle boil. Cook, stirring constantly, until the mixture is thickened (it should coat the back of a wooden spoon), 1–2 minutes.

Pour enough sauce over the omelets until it pools a little on the plate. Serve immediately with steamed rice and a meat or vegetable side dish.

Vegetables

Although abundant, vegetables aren't a highlight of the Indonesian diet. Common vegetables include pakis (ferns), the leaves of plants grown for their fruit and tubers—like papaya and tapioca—and easy-to-grow kangkung (water spinach), cucumbers, and long beans. And of course, there are Dutch imports like tomatoes, potatoes, cabbage, and carrots, which are grown in elevated areas rich in volcanic soil and suited to temperate vegetables.

The simplest way to add vegetables to a meal—and Julia's favorite—is to have Lalapan (page 94), fresh local vegetables eaten with sambal. In Indonesia, the most commonly eaten vegetables include cucumber, lettuce, kemangi (lemon basil), long beans, and tomatoes because they are inexpensive and available year-round. But they can vary by region. The vegetables are usually served raw but are sometimes blanched or grilled.

My go-to vegetable dish is a quick stir-fry like Cap Cay (page 93), using whatever vegetables I have on hand. This is one example of a typical vegetable dish that isn't completely vegetarian: shrimp paste, small amounts of meat, and seafood are often added. There are many terms for stir-fry—*oseng oseng, tumis, orak arik,* and *cah*—but they all mean basically the same thing.

Mixed Vegetable and Seafood Stir-Fry

CAP CAY

Makes 4–6 servings as part of a multicourse meal

2 tablespoons vegetable oil

2 cloves garlic, minced

1 carrot, sliced thinly on the diagonal

2 cups (115 g) cauliflower florets

4 napa cabbage leaves, chopped and stems and leaves separated

¼ cup (60 ml) low-sodium chicken stock or water, plus more as needed

1 cup (160 g) snow peas, halved if large

½ red bell pepper, cut into 1-inch (2.5-cm) squares

8 fish balls (3½ oz/100 g), quartered

3 oz (90 g) large (31/35) raw shrimp, peeled and deveined

2 tablespoons oyster sauce

Dash fish sauce or soy sauce

½ small yellow onion, sliced

2 green onions, cut into 2-inch (5-cm) lengths

1 teaspoon cornstarch

2 tablespoons water

Cap cay (pronounced "chup chai"), sometimes spelled *cap cai*, is the Hokkien-derived term for this popular stir-fried vegetable dish that originates from Fujian cuisine. It is a dish that my dad, Rudy, often requests. It isn't traditionally a vegetarian dish, as meat (usually chicken) and/or seafood are often added to the mix. But feel free to omit if preferred. You can use any vegetable you'd like. Some of our favorites include leeks, broccoli, bok choy, green cabbage, tomatoes, mushrooms, and baby corn.

Heat the oil in a wok or large, heavy skillet over medium-high heat until shimmering hot. Fry the garlic until fragrant, about 30 seconds. Add the carrot, cauliflower, and cabbage stems. Stir and cook for about 4 minutes. Add the chicken stock to prevent the vegetables from burning.

Add the snow peas, bell pepper, and cabbage leaves, stirring in between each addition. Add more stock or water a little at a time, up to ¼ cup (60 ml), as necessary to prevent the vegetables from burning.

When the veggies are tender, reduce the heat to medium. Add the fish balls and shrimp and stir and cook until the shrimp curl and just turn pink, 30 seconds to 1 minute. Season with the oyster sauce and a dash of fish sauce. The dish should be saucy. Add more stock or water, 1 tablespoon at a time, if necessary. Taste and adjust the seasonings if desired.

Toss in the yellow onion and green onions. In a small bowl, combine the cornstarch and water to create a slurry. Stir in the slurry and cook until the sauce thickens, 1–2 minutes.

Serve immediately with steamed rice and a protein dish.

Vegetable Crudités Dipped in Sambal

LALAPAN

Makes 4–6 servings as part of a multicourse meal

2 Roma tomatoes quartered

1 cucumber, sliced or cut into spears

¼ lb (115 g) green beans, blanched

1 chayote, peeled, seeded, cut into wedges, and blanched

4 cabbage leaves, chopped into 2–3 inch (5–7.5 cm) squares and blanched

1 carrot, peeled and cut into sticks

Handful lemon basil leaves or Thai basil leaves

½ cup (120 ml) sambal of your choice

NOTES
Other vegetables to consider include eggplant, boiled spinach, bell peppers, winged beans, romaine lettuce, and petal, if you dare!

Lalapan is a Sundanese salad that comprises an assortment of raw and cooked vegetables usually served with sambal terasi. It is a unique Indonesian dining experience and an easy way to include vegetables in a meal. Lalapan often accompanies fried or grilled meat and seafood dishes and acts as a palate cleanser to counter the richness of a meal. For Julia and many Indonesians, lalapan makes a meal complete.

There are no hard-and-fast rules for which vegetables and sambal are appropriate for lalapan. This recipe includes some of Julia's favorite vegetables—with the exception of hard-to-find, and swallow, petai (stink beans). Feel free to choose whatever ones you like and dip them in your favorite sambal. My sambal of choice is Julia's Sambal Terasi (page 169)!

Arrange the tomatoes, cucumber, green beans, chayote, cabbage, carrot, and basil on a serving platter. Serve with a bowl of the sambal to accompany Ayam Goreng Kuning (page 51), Ayam Panggang Kecap (page 128), or Ikan Bakar (page 75).

To eat, dip a vegetable into the sambal. Or dab a little sambal onto the vegetable with a spoon.

NOTES
Pan-fry 6 hard-cooked eggs in a little oil until blistered and brown. Toss with the sambal.

Spread the sambal over 1 lb (450 g) of salmon fillets seasoned with salt and white pepper. Roast in a preheated 400°F (200°C) oven for 4–6 minutes per inch for medium-rare (or until cooked to your liking).

Spicy Eggplant

TERUNG BALADO

Makes 4 servings as part of a multicourse meal

3 tablespoons vegetable oil, plus more for greasing and drizzling, divided

1 lb (450 g) Chinese or Japanese eggplant, cut into 2-inch (5-cm) batons and patted dry

1 teaspoon coriander seeds or ground coriander

4 small Asian shallots or 2 large European shallots, chopped

2 cloves garlic, smashed

4 medium-hot finger-length red chilies, such as Fresno, cayenne, or serrano, seeded (optional) and chopped, or 2 tablespoons sambal oelek

2 red bird's eye chilies or Thai chilies, stemmed, seeded, and chopped (optional)

1 small red bell pepper, chopped

1 teaspoon fine sea salt

4 makrut lime leaves

1 (½-inch/12-mm) slice galangal

1 stalk lemongrass, trimmed and bruised

1 large tomato, chopped

2 teaspoons sugar

Juice of 1 key lime

The spicy sauce in this recipe is technically a sambal, and this dish is a great example of how versatile a sambal can be! It's not just a condiment but can be used as a flavoring paste as well. While you can cook many foods the "balado" way, eggplant is my favorite. I try to use Asian varieties of eggplant, which contain fewer seeds than Italian globe eggplants and are less bitter. Chinese (light purple) or Japanese (dark purple) eggplant have thin skins and don't necessarily have to be salted, but soaking in salted water does prevent browning. If using Italian eggplant, salt the pieces to remove bitterness and peel if the skin is thick. Feel free to pan-fry the eggplant (1 minute), microwave on high (4 minutes), or boil (8 minutes).

Preheat the oven to 450°F (230°C). Grease a large baking sheet with oil.

Arrange the eggplant in a single layer on the prepared baking sheet and drizzle with more oil. Roast for 12–14 minutes, flipping once, until soft but not completely cooked through.

Meanwhile, make the sambal: Toast the coriander seeds in a small, dry skillet over medium heat until fragrant and browned, 5–6 minutes. Grind into a coarse powder with a spice grinder or mortar and pestle.

In a small food processor or blender, pulse the coriander, shallots, garlic, finger-length chilies, bird's eye chilies (if using), bell pepper, and salt with 1 tablespoon of oil until the texture of oatmeal, about 1 minute. Scrape down the sides of the bowl as necessary. Or use a mortar and pestle. You should have about 1 cup (240 ml) of sambal.

Heat the remaining 2 tablespoons of oil in a wok or large, heavy skillet over medium heat until shimmering hot. Add the sambal, lime leaves, galangal, and lemongrass and stir and cook until fragrant, 5–7 minutes. Reduce the heat if the paste is browning too fast; you don't want it to burn. Add the tomato and stir to mix. Simmer until the tomatoes wilt, 6–8 minutes. Add the sugar and lime juice. Taste and adjust the seasonings if desired.

Add the partially cooked eggplant and stir to mix. Simmer until the eggplant is cooked through and has absorbed some of the sauce, 1–2 minutes. Remove the lime leaves, lemongrass, and galangal.

Serve with steamed rice and a meat dish like Ayam Goreng Kuning (page 51).

Spicy Stir-Fried Water Spinach

SAMBAL KANGKUNG

Makes 4 servings as part of a multicourse meal

2 tablespoons vegetable oil

3 Asian shallots or 1 European shallot, minced

3 cloves garlic, minced

1 medium-hot finger-length red chili, such as Fresno, cayenne, or serrano, seeded (optional) and thinly sliced

½ teaspoon fine sea salt

1 tablespoon dried shrimp, soaked in water for 10 minutes, patted dry, and minced (optional)

3 tablespoons Julia's Sambal Terasi (page 169)

1 teaspoon sugar

1 bundle (¾ lb/340 g) leafy greens, such as kangkung, garland chrysanthemum, or mature spinach, tough ends trimmed, stems and leaves separated and chopped into 2–3 inch (5–7.5 cm) pieces (see notes)

1 large tomato, sliced into 8 wedges

Kangkung is a long, leafy green vegetable with hollow stems that is popular in Southeast Asia. However, it's not easy to find in the United States, even at Asian markets. Thankfully, I've found that chrysanthemum greens (garland chrysanthemum) make a wonderful substitute. It has a similar sweet and nutty flavor as well as the same sturdy texture. However, you can use any green leafy vegetable (I prefer Asian vegetables like choy sum or yu choy) for this recipe. Just adjust cooking times for softer vegetables like spinach. You can also substitute the sambal terasi with sambal oelek, or omit the sambal altogether if you don't like it spicy.

Heat the oil in a wok or large, heavy skillet over medium heat until shimmering hot. Add the shallots, garlic, chili, and salt and stir and cook until fragrant, about 1 minute. Stir in the dried shrimp (if using) and cook for 30 seconds.

Add the sambal terasi and sugar and stir until fragrant. Add the kangkung stems and stir and cook until they are soft but haven't lost their crunch, about 2 minutes. Add the leaves and stir and cook until wilted, 1–2 minutes. Add the tomato wedges and stir and cook until they are soft and release their juices.

The kangkung will release some liquid but add a little water (about ¼ cup/60 ml) to make a shallow puddle if necessary. Add the tomato wedges and stir to heat through. Serve with steamed rice and a meat dish.

NOTES

Kangkung is a semiaquatic vegetable, growing in rice fields. Thus, it contains a lot of grit. Trim 1–2 inches (2.5–5 cm) from the tough ends and discard. Pick out and discard any leaves that aren't fresh and vibrant green.

Cut the remaining kangkung into 2–3 inch (5–7.5 cm) lengths. Transfer them to a large basin of cold water. They should be fully submerged to clean them properly. Use your hands to agitate the water and the vegetables to shake out any grit. Soak for 5–10 minutes to allow any dirt or sand particles to settle.

Gently lift the kangkung out of the water to a colander. Discard the sandy water, and repeat the process 1–2 times, until the vegetables are clean.

Vegetables and Shrimp Fried in Sambal

SAMBAL GORENG SAYUR UDANG

Makes 4–6 servings as part of a multicourse meal

FOR THE SPICE PASTE

3 candlenuts or unsalted macadamias

1 teaspoon coriander seeds or ground coriander

4 Asian shallots or 2 European shallots

4–6 medium-hot finger-length red chilies, such as Fresno, cayenne, or serrano, seeded (optional) and chopped, or 1–2 tablespoons sambal oelek

2 cloves garlic, smashed

1 teaspoon ground turmeric

1 teaspoon Terasi Bakar (page 189) or anchovy paste (optional)

3 tablespoons vegetable oil, divided

5 (½-inch/12-mm) slices galangal

3 salam leaves or makrut lime leaves

1 stalk lemongrass, trimmed and bruised

1 cup (240 ml) unsweetened coconut milk

1 chayote, peeled and chopped into bite-size pieces

½ lb (225 g) green beans or French beans, cut into 2-inch (5-cm) pieces

½ lb (225 g) fried tofu, store-bought or homemade (page 83), cut into 2 × 1-inch (5 × 2.5-cm) rectangles

2 teaspoons sugar

1 teaspoon fine sea salt

6 oz (170 g) medium (41/50) raw shrimp, peeled and deveined

Sambal goreng simply means "fried spice paste" and refers to a whole class of dishes featuring a dizzying array of meat and vegetables— sambal goreng ayam (chicken), sambal goreng tahu (tofu), and the list goes on. This one is usually a much brighter red because of the amount of chilies used, but I'm a wuss when it comes to spice. Feel free to add more if you'd like. Julia loves adding petai (stink bean) if she can find it. Petai, tofu, and shrimp is the most popular combo of sambal goreng ingredients. No points for guessing why I haven't included the stink bean! To make this dish vegetarian, omit the shrimp and terasi bakar (shrimp paste).

———

To make the spice paste, toast the candlenuts and coriander seeds separately in a small, dry skillet over medium heat until fragrant and browned, 5–6 minutes each. Crush the candlenuts with the flat part of a knife's blade. Grind the coriander into a coarse powder with a spice grinder or mortar and pestle. (If using ground coriander, just add it to the food processor in the next step.)

In a small food processor or blender, pulse the candlenuts, coriander, shallots, chilies, garlic, turmeric, and terasi bakar (if using) with 1 tablespoon of oil until the texture of oatmeal, about 1 minute. Scrape down the sides of the bowl as necessary. Or use a mortar and pestle.

Heat the remaining 2 tablespoons of oil in a large, heavy skillet over medium heat until shimmering hot. Add the spice paste, galangal, salam leaves, and lemongrass and stir and cook until it is very fragrant and has turned a few shades darker (this indicates the shallots are caramelizing), 5–7 minutes. Reduce the heat if the paste is browning too fast; you don't want the paste to burn. Once the moisture has evaporated, the ingredients will separate from the oil. The paste is now ready for the next step.

Stir in the coconut milk and 1 cup (240 ml) water. Add the chayote, green beans, and tofu. Simmer for about 15 minutes, or until the vegetables are cooked to your liking, stirring occasionally. Season with the sugar and salt. Taste and adjust the seasonings if desired.

Add the shrimp and stir and cook until they just turn pink, 1–2 minutes. Remove from the heat immediately and serve with steamed rice or as part of Lontong Cap Go Meh (page 183).

Young Jackfruit Stew

GUDEG

Makes 6–8 servings as part of a multicourse meal

3 cans (20 oz/570 g each) young unripe jackfruit in brine, rinsed, drained, and cut into bite-size pieces

2 cups (475 ml) coconut water or water, divided

1½ cups (350 ml) unsweetened coconut milk, divided

4 salam leaves or makrut lime leaves

6 (½-inch/12-mm) slices galangal, divided

5 candlenuts or unsalted macadamias

2 tablespoons coriander seeds or ground coriander

10 Asian shallots or 5 European shallots

5 cloves garlic, smashed

3 teaspoons fine sea salt, divided

1 tablespoon vegetable oil

½ cup (80 g) shaved palm sugar or brown sugar, plus more as needed

3 tablespoons kecap manis

1 tablespoon mushroom seasoning powder (optional)

½ teaspoon ground white or black pepper

1 stalk lemongrass, trimmed and bruised

6 large hard-boiled eggs (optional)

Gudeg, young jackfruit braised in coconut milk and spices, is a traditional Central Javanese dish. Unlike the other dishes in this book, Julia did not make gudeg at home. In fact, I had gudeg for the first time in Yogyakarta when I was eleven years old. I remember sitting on plastic mats on the ground. I remember a toothless old lady wearing a sarong kebaya and a tight bun on her head. And I remember that lingering first bite. When I was back in Yogya in the summer of 2022, I jumped at the chance to learn how to make gudeg from acclaimed vegan chef Dewi Novita Sari. Dewi, who runs the plant-based restaurant Little Garden with her husband, Dadang Herry Murpiyanto, opened her home kitchen to teach me how to make gudeg and several other dishes. This recipe is an adaption of the one she shared with me.

Like many Javanese dishes, gudeg is meant to be super sweet, but feel free to rein in the sugar by adding less or skipping the kecap manis. You may notice that this recipe makes a large portion, and that's intentional. Since making gudeg takes about two hours, I want to make it worthwhile! Take heart, gudeg freezes well and can keep for up to a month.

Combine the jackfruit, 1½ cups (350 ml) of coconut water, ½ cup (120 ml) of coconut milk, the salam leaves, and 3 slices of galangal in a wok or large, heavy pot and simmer over medium-low heat for 30 minutes. Stir occasionally, scooping the soup up high and pouring it back into the pan. Don't let it boil or the coconut milk will split.

While the jackfruit is simmering, make the spice paste: toast the candlenuts and coriander seeds separately in a small, dry skillet over medium heat until fragrant and browned, 5–6 minutes each. Crush the candlenuts with the flat part of a knife's blade. Grind the coriander into a coarse powder with a spice grinder or mortar and pestle. (If using ground coriander, just add it to the food processor in the next step.)

In a small food processor or blender, pulse the candlenuts, coriander, shallots, garlic, and 1 teaspoon of salt with the oil until the texture of oatmeal, about 1 minute. Scrape down the sides of the bowl as necessary. Or use a mortar and pestle. (If using a mortar and pestle, grind the coriander first, then add the rest of the ingredients one by one with a pinch of salt.)

Recipe continues

NOTES

To use an electric pressure cooker, Pressure cook on high for 45 minutes and release the steam naturally. Then cook on Sauté until the stew is almost dry.

In Indonesia, you can buy fresh young jackfruit already peeled and chopped at the market. Canned jackfruit is a good alternative. I wouldn't recommend trying to process fresh jackfruit on your own (whether unripe or ripe). It has a sticky sap that is difficult to remove.

Try using oyster mushrooms or banana blossoms in place of jackfruit in this recipe.

Add the spice paste, palm sugar, kecap manis, remaining 2 teaspoons of salt, the mushroom powder (if using), white pepper, lemongrass, remaining 3 galangal slices, and remaining ½ cup (120 ml) of coconut water to the pot with the jackfruit. Keep stirring over medium heat until the liquid is mostly absorbed, about 15 minutes. Add the remaining 1 cup (240 ml) of coconut milk and the eggs (if using).

Reduce the heat to the lowest setting possible and simmer, covered, until the jackfruit has absorbed the flavors and is soft and tender enough to pull apart with a fork, 1½–2 hours. Taste and add more sugar if you'd like it sweeter (I added 2 tablespoons more) and adjust the other seasonings as desired. Fish out the herbs and discard.

The gudeg is now ready to eat but will be even tastier the next day. Serve with steamed rice and Opor Ayam Putih (page 56).

One-dish meals, featuring carbs, protein, and vegetables all in a single dish, often equate to comfort food. And Indonesian comfort foods can have rice, noodles, and even vegetables at the core. They can be quick and easy to prepare, or they can be a little more involved, such as Nasi Bakmoy (page 109). They can feed two people for a weeknight meal with leftovers to bring to work, such as Mi Goreng (page 110). Or they can be scaled up to feed a party of a dozen or more, such as Bakmi Jamur (page 113)! Regardless, there is a one-dish meal to suit every occasion.

Many of the dishes in this chapter are perfect for everyday cooking. Take Spicy Sheet Pan Fried Rice (page 106), for instance. Using leftovers, it's a cinch to make

Chapter 3

One-Dish Meals

Makanan Sederhana

Much like a salad bowl in the West, vegetables and peanut sauce make for a classic Indonesian one-dish meal. Regional variations abound. Some like the vegetables raw. Others like them boiled. Sometimes the peanut sauce is spiked with lots of vinegar and/or garlic. Often, ingredients like potatoes, tofu, or egg are added. Regardless, this combination provides an easy-to-prepare, satisfying, and nutritious meal. The most filling of them is Siomay Bandung (page 125), in which tofu and vegetables are stuffed with fish or meat paste.

Spicy Sheet Pan Fried Rice

NASI GORENG

Makes 4 servings

½ lb (225 g) boneless, skinless chicken thighs, cut into ½-inch (12-mm) cubes

2 cloves garlic, minced

2 Asian shallots or 1 European shallot, minced

1 tablespoon oyster sauce

½ teaspoon fine sea salt, plus more as needed

½ teaspoon ground white or black pepper, plus more as needed

2–3 tablespoons vegetable oil, divided

1 red or green bell pepper, cut into ¼-inch (6-mm) squares

¼ lb (115 g) fresh button mushrooms, stemmed and sliced

¼ lb (115 g) green or Chinese cabbage, shredded

2 tablespoons kecap manis

1 tablespoon sambal terasi or sambal oelek

1 tablespoon fish sauce

4 heaping cups (625 g) day-old or chilled cooked jasmine or other polished long-grain rice

1 cup (140 g) frozen peas, thawed

4 fried eggs (page 81, optional)

Fried shallots for serving

Sambal for serving

Acar Campur (page 172) for serving

Oma says:
Start frying the eggs about 5 minutes before you expect the rice to be done.

Julia often made nasi goreng, the Indonesian version of fried rice, when we were growing up. It's every working mom's dream dish: fast to prepare, endlessly adaptable, and a great way to use up leftovers. We had it for breakfast, lunch, and dinner. Making nasi goreng the traditional way (on the stove top) isn't hard, but this sheet pan version is an excellent alternative. It uses the oven for the heavy lifting and produces the perfect amount of crisping, achieving the characteristic "burnt" flavor so elusive in home kitchens.

Toss together the chicken, garlic, and shallots with the oyster sauce, ½ teaspoon salt, and ½ teaspoon white pepper in a large bowl.

Preheat the oven to 450°F (230°C). Line a large rimmed baking sheet with aluminum foil, then drizzle with 1 tablespoon of oil.

Transfer the marinated chicken mixture to the prepared baking sheet and roast for 5 minutes. Remove the baking sheet from the oven and stir. Return to the oven and roast until the chicken is no longer pink, 2–3 minutes longer.

Add the bell pepper, mushrooms, and cabbage to the baking sheet. Sprinkle lightly with salt and stir well to coat with the oil, adding up to 1 tablespoon more oil as necessary. Roast until the vegetables have wilted, about 10 minutes, stirring halfway through cooking.

Whisk together the kecap manis, sambal, fish sauce, and remaining 1 tablespoon of oil in a large bowl. Add the rice and mix until coated.

Remove the baking sheet from the oven. Stir the rice into the meat and vegetables and press down on everything with the back of a spatula. Return to the oven and cook until the rice starts to crisp on the bottom, 20–25 minutes. Halfway through, add the peas, stir to mix, and press down again. Taste and season with more salt and white pepper if desired.

Divide the oven-fried rice among 4 plates or bowls and top each portion with a fried egg (if using). Sprinkle with fried shallots and serve immediately with sambal and acar campur.

Chicken Rice Porridge

BUBUR AYAM

Makes 4 servings

6 cups (1.4 L) water

3 cups (470 g) cooked white rice, any type is fine

½ lb (225 g) bone-in, skinless chicken thighs

3 (¼-inch/6-mm) slices fresh ginger

1 clove garlic, smashed

1 green onion, knotted

½ small yellow onion, peeled

2 tablespoons soy sauce

1 teaspoon fine sea salt

½ teaspoon ground white or black pepper

¼ cup (20 g) chopped green onions

FOR SERVING

Fried shallots

Fried garlic (optional)

Sesame oil

Kecap manis

NOTES

If you don't already have cooked rice in your fridge, use 1 cup (200 g) of uncooked rice (beras). You'll have to extend the total cooking time to 1½–2 hours.

Oma says:
Use broken rice. The bubur will be so thick and creamy and takes a shorter time to cook. Also, broken rice is cheaper!

Like chicken noodle soup, chicken rice porridge, also called congee, is a panacea for all ills. Personally, I don't just reserve it for when I'm sick. I can eat rice porridge anytime: for breakfast, on a chilly winter's day, or whenever I miss Julia and her cooking. This is the bare bones recipe, but I can go crazy with the toppings. I'll add barbecue pork, dried scallops, century egg, pork floss, pickles, and so on. Sometimes, I'll crack a raw egg into my steaming bowl of porridge and stir continuously, allowing the inherent heat to cook the egg. If I have some on hand, I add small cubes of sweet potato toward the end of cooking to lend sweetness and texture to the final dish.

In a large pot, combine the water, rice, chicken, ginger, garlic, knotted green onion, and yellow onion. Bring to a boil over high heat. Skim off any scum or foam that rises to the surface.

Reduce the heat to low. Cover and simmer, stirring occasionally so that the rice doesn't stick to the bottom of the pot, for 20 minutes. Pull out the chicken, scrape the meat off the bones, and set aside. Return the bones to the pot and continue cooking, stirring occasionally, for about 40 minutes longer, until the rice grains are swollen and the mixture is as thick as oatmeal. Meanwhile, shred or chop the meat and set aside for later.

If the porridge is too thick, add more water. If it's too thin, cook it until it reaches the desired smoothness and thickness.

Remove the bones, ginger, garlic, green onion, and yellow onion. Add the soy sauce, salt, and white pepper. Taste and adjust the seasonings if desired.

Ladle the porridge into individual bowls, top with the shredded chicken, green onions, fried shallots, and fried garlic (if using). Serve with sesame oil and kecap manis for drizzling.

You can also make congee in an electric pressure cooker. Cook on High pressure for 20 minutes and allow it to release pressure naturally. Stir the congee, adding more water if you'd like a thinner porridge.

Meat, Tofu, and Soup over Rice

NASI BAKMOY

Makes 6 servings

1½ lb (680 g) bone-in, skinless chicken thighs

½ lb (225 g) raw head-on, tail-on shrimp

8 cups (1.9 L) water

3 tablespoons fish sauce, divided

1 teaspoon fine sea salt

1½ teaspoons ground pepper

3 tablespoons vegetable oil

3 cloves garlic, minced

1½ cups (170 g) chopped yellow onion

¼ cup (60 ml) kecap manis

2 tablespoons oyster sauce

½ lb (225 g) fried tofu, cut into ½-inch (12-mm) pieces

¼ lb (115 g) button mushrooms, chopped

4 fish balls (¼ lb/115 g), cut into bite-size pieces (optional)

6 cups (1 kg) cooked white long-grain rice

12 hard-boiled quail eggs or 3 chicken eggs, halved (optional)

¼ cup (20 g) chopped green onions

¼ cup (15 g) chopped Chinese celery leaves or parsley

Fried shallots for serving

Fried garlic for serving (optional)

Oma says:
If you have meat-tofu mixture left over, blanch chopped green beans until barely cooked. Then stir-fry with the mixture and serve with steamed rice.

A bowl of *nasi bakmoy* has three parts to it: scoop of rice, savory topping, and soup. Every time Julia makes it, she seems to use a different combination of ingredients for the topping. So feel free to swap the chicken for pork shoulder or pork belly, and use more shrimp instead of fish balls. I like to buy bone-in meat and reserve the bones to make stock. If you choose to buy chicken stock, you will need 3 oz (90 g) raw peeled shrimp and 1 lb (450 g) boneless, skinless chicken meat instead.

Debone the chicken and peel the shrimp. Reserve the bones and shrimp heads and shells to make the stock. Dice the chicken into ½-inch (12-mm) cubes and cut the shrimp into a similar size.

To prepare the soup, combine the chicken bones, shrimp heads and shells, and water in a large pot. Bring to a boil over high heat. Reduce the heat to medium-low and simmer, covered, for 1 hour. Strain the soup and discard the solids, then season the soup with 1 tablespoon of fish sauce, the salt, and ½ teaspoon of pepper. Taste and adjust the seasonings if desired. You don't want it to be too salty because it is served with the meat-tofu topping, which is also seasoned.

Heat the oil in a wok or large, heavy skillet over medium heat until shimmering hot. Add the garlic and yellow onion and stir and cook until fragrant and the onion is translucent, 2–3 minutes. Add the chicken and stir and cook until the chicken is no longer pink, about 2 minutes. Add the kecap manis, oyster sauce, remaining 2 tablespoons of fish sauce, and remaining teaspoon of pepper. Stir to mix, then add the tofu, mushrooms, shrimp, and fish balls (if using). Reduce the heat to medium-low and simmer until the ingredients are cooked through and the flavors have melded, 10–15 minutes longer. Taste and adjust the seasonings if desired. It should be a little sweet and a little salty.

To serve, scoop 1 cup (155 g) of cooked rice into each bowl. Top with ½–¾ cup (115–170 g) of meat-tofu mixture and 2 quail eggs or ½ chicken egg (if using). Pour about 1 cup (240 ml) of soup into each bowl. Shower with the green onions, celery leaves, fried shallots, and fried garlic (if using).

Fried Noodles

MI GORENG

½ lb (225 g) boneless, skinless chicken thighs or breasts, cut into bite-size pieces

2 tablespoons oyster sauce or soy sauce

½ lb (225 g) dried or 1 lb (450 g) fresh, cooked egg or wheat noodles, any shape or size

½ lb (225 g) bok choy or other leafy greens, such as choy sum, yu choy, or Swiss chard

5 tablespoons (75 ml) vegetable oil, divided, plus more as needed

3 cloves garlic, minced

½ small yellow onion, thinly sliced

1 carrot, peeled and thinly sliced

2 large eggs, beaten

3 tablespoons kecap manis

2 tablespoons fish sauce or soy sauce

½ teaspoon ground white or black pepper

FOR SERVING

Fried shallots

Chopped green onions

Chopped Chinese celery leaves or parsley

Shrimp crackers or store-bought veggie chips

Like Nasi Goreng (page 106), mi goreng is a dish I never *plan* to make. That being said, I always have a stash of dried noodles in my pantry. Julia, on the other hand, always has fresh noodles lurking in the fridge or freezer. In a pinch, you can even use instant noodles. And if you're gluten-free, rice noodles are always an option. Good candidates for ingredients include chopped leftover rotisserie chicken or ham (about 1½ cups/250 g), or substitute another protein like tofu, shrimp, or fish/beef balls. Have all the ingredients prepped and ready to go when you start cooking—it will go fast!

Marinate the chicken with the oyster sauce in a medium bowl while you prepare the other ingredients.

If using dried noodles, cook for 1 minute less than the package instructions. If using fresh, cooked noodles, rinse with boiling water and separate the strands. Drain and set aside.

Trim the bottom inch from the head of bok choy. Cut the thick white stems just below the leafy green portion. Stack a few stems at a time and chop them crosswise into ¼-inch (6-mm) pieces. Stack the leafy greens and cut them crosswise into ½-inch (12-mm) pieces. Keep the stems and leaves separated. The stems will be added first because they take longer to cook. You will get a total of about 3 cups (250 g).

Heat 2 tablespoons of oil in a wok or large, heavy pan over medium-high heat until shimmering hot. Add the garlic and yellow onion and stir and cook until fragrant, about 30 seconds. Add the bok choy stems and carrot and stir and cook until wilted, 1–2 minutes.

Push the veggies to one side of the pan and add 1 tablespoon of oil. Spread the chicken out in a single layer. Sear for about 2 minutes, then flip and cook on the other side until most of the pink is gone, 1–2 minutes longer. Mix everything together and push to one side of the pan.

Add the remaining 2 tablespoons of oil and pour in the beaten eggs. Allow the eggs to set for about 1 minute before scrambling. Add the bok choy leaves and stir everything (including the ingredients on the side) together until the leaves wilt, 1–2 minutes. Add a bit more oil if the ingredients start sticking to the pan. Season with the kecap manis, fish sauce, and white pepper, stirring everything continuously.

NOTES
If you don't have a wok or large pan (I recommend at least 12 inches/30 cm), or just prefer it, you can cook the ingredients separately and transfer the cooked foods to a plate at each stage, then combine them together at the end.

Add the noodles to the pan, stir to combine with the rest of the ingredients, and heat everything through. At this point I like to use tongs to mix everything thoroughly. Taste and adjust the seasonings if desired.

Divide the noodles among 4–6 serving plates and shower with fried shallots, green onions, and celery leaves. Serve immediately with shrimp crackers.

Pork and Mushroom Noodles

BAKMI JAMUR

Makes 6–8 servings

4 tablespoons (60 ml) vegetable oil, divided

3 cloves garlic, minced

1 yellow onion, finely chopped

1½ lb (680 g) ground pork, chicken, or turkey

½ lb (225 g) cremini mushrooms, sliced, or 1 can (15 oz/425 g) straw mushrooms, drained

¼ cup (60 ml) kecap manis, plus more for serving

2 tablespoons soy sauce

2 tablespoons fish sauce, divided

1 teaspoon ground pepper, plus more to taste

2 packages (1 lb/450 g each) frozen fish balls or meatballs, thawed

6 cups (1.4 L) low-sodium chicken stock

Fine sea salt to taste

1 bunch (¾ lb/340 g) baby bok choy, leaves separated, or other leafy greens

1 lb (450 g) dried thin or wide wheat noodles or 2 lb (1 kg) fresh noodles

2 green onions, chopped, plus more for garnish

3 tablespoons fried shallots, plus more for garnish

Sambal oelek for serving

Tomato ketchup for serving

NOTES

Fish balls and meatballs (made with fish or meat and a binder like tapioca starch) are sold in the frozen section of Asian markets.

Bakmi jamur—noodles topped with pork and mushrooms and sometimes served with fish balls or meatballs—is one of my favorite comfort foods. My siblings and I ate this dish as often as an American kid might eat spaghetti. I've always wondered where this dish came from, and in 2022, I got my answer upon my return to Jakarta. When Julia and my dad, Rudy, were dating in the 1960s, they would go to Bakmi Aboen, a hole-in-the-wall eatery at the end of an alley in Jakarta's Pasar Baru district. The restaurant is still there, and the menu remains the same, including bakmi jamur.

Heat 3 tablespoons of oil in a wok or large, heavy skillet over medium-high heat until shimmering hot. Add the garlic and yellow onion and stir and cook until the onion softens and is translucent, 2–3 minutes.

Add the pork and stir and cook until no longer pink, 3–5 minutes. Add the mushrooms and stir until soft, 1–2 minutes. Add the kecap manis, soy sauce, 1 tablespoon of fish sauce, and the white pepper, stirring to mix. Taste and adjust the seasonings if desired. Adjust the heat to medium-low and simmer, covered, for 30 minutes.

Combine the fish balls and stock in a medium pot and simmer over medium heat for 10 minutes, until warmed through. Season with salt and white pepper to taste.

Bring a large pot of water to a boil. Blanch the bok choy until it just turns bright green, about 1 minute. Remove with tongs and set aside. Bring the water to a boil again and cook the noodles according to package directions. Drain in a colander and rinse with cold water to stop further cooking. Transfer the noodles to a large bowl and drizzle with the remaining 1 tablespoon of oil and remaining 1 tablespoon of fish sauce. Sprinkle with the green onions and fried shallots, tossing to coat.

Divide the noodles among 6–8 individual bowls. Spoon about ½ cup (115 g) of the pork-mushroom mixture over the noodles and top with bok choy. Shower the noodles with more green onions and fried shallots. Ladle ½ cup (120 ml) of soup and 2–3 fish balls into small bowls to serve on the side and sprinkle with green onions. Serve with sambal, tomato ketchup, and more kecap manis.

To eat, you can have the noodles dry, squirting sambal, tomato ketchup, or kecap manis over them and dipping the fish balls in any of the sauces. Alternatively, you can pour the soup over the noodles for a soupy dish.

Indonesian Shepherd's Pie

PASTEL PANGGANG

Makes 4–6 servings

FOR THE TOPPING

1¼ lb (570 g) yellow gold potatoes, peeled and quartered

1½ teaspoons fine sea salt

2 tablespoons unsalted butter

¼ cup (60 ml) whole milk

½ teaspoon ground nutmeg

¼ teaspoon ground white pepper

2 large egg yolks

¼ cup (7 g) Chinese celery leaves or parsley, finely chopped

FOR THE FILLING

2 tablespoons unsalted butter

6 Asian shallots or 3 European shallots, minced

3 cloves garlic, minced

2 tablespoons all-purpose flour

½ cup (120 ml) whole milk

½ cup (120 ml) chicken stock

1½ cups (250 g) diced cooked chicken

1 cup (170 g) chopped ham

2 oz (60 g) bean thread noodles, soaked in hot water and roughly cut

½ cup (15 g) dried wood ear mushrooms, soaked in hot water and chopped

1 teaspoon fine sea salt

1 teaspoon sugar

½ teaspoon ground pepper

½ teaspoon ground nutmeg

1 cup (140 g) frozen mixed vegetables, thawed

2 large hard-boiled eggs, sliced

1 large egg yolk + 1 tablespoon water to make an egg wash

The Dutch influence in this dish that was once called Indische pastel (a name rarely used anymore) is palpable—hello, mashed potato topping! But the filling, with oddities like bean thread noodles and wood ear mushrooms, also makes it very Indonesian. Leave them out if you prefer.

To make the mashed potato topping, place the potatoes in a large saucepan and add enough cold water to cover by at least 1 inch (2.5 cm). Add ½ teaspoon of salt. Bring to a boil over high heat, then reduce the heat to low and simmer, covered, until fork-tender, 15–20 minutes.

Drain the potatoes in a colander. While they are still hot, press them through a ricer into a large bowl, or mash them with a potato masher or large fork. Stir in the butter until completely melted. Then pour in the milk, stirring continuously. Add the remaining 1 teaspoon of salt, the nutmeg, and pepper and mix. Taste and adjust the seasonings if desired. Add the egg yolks and celery leaves, then stir with a sturdy wooden spoon until the potatoes are smooth. Don't overstir or you'll end up with gluey mashed potatoes. Set aside.

Preheat the oven to 350°F (180°C).

To make the filling, melt the butter in a wok or large, heavy skillet over medium heat. Fry the shallots and garlic until fragrant, about 1 minute. Sprinkle in the flour and stir until a thick paste forms, about 1 minute. Continue stirring while you pour the milk and stock into the pan. Keep stirring until there are no more lumps. Add the chicken, ham, bean thread noodles, mushrooms, salt, sugar, pepper, and nutmeg. Stir and cook until the sauce thickens, 2–3 minutes. Stir in the mixed vegetables. Taste and adjust the seasonings if desired.

Transfer the filling to an 11 × 7-inch (28 × 18-cm) glass or ceramic baking dish. Arrange the cooked egg slices on top. Spread the mashed potatoes evenly over the filling, starting from the edges to create a seal and prevent the filling from bubbling up. Smooth with a rubber spatula.

Brush the topping with the egg wash. Use a fork to make crisscross patterns across the top. Place on a rimmed baking sheet (to catch spills) and bake for 30–40 minutes, until the top is golden brown. Allow to stand for 15 minutes before serving.

Spicy Stir-Fried Rice Vermicelli

MEE SIAM

Makes 4-6 servings

10 oz (285 g) rice vermicelli

12 Asian shallots or 6 European shallots, chopped

6 cloves garlic, smashed

4 medium-hot finger-length red chilies, such as Fresno, cayenne, or serrano, seeded (optional) and chopped

½ cup (20 g) dried shrimp, soaked and drained (optional)

3 tablespoons yellow bean sauce or tauco

1 teaspoon Terasi Bakar (page 189, optional)

3 tablespoons vegetable oil, divided

½ lb (225 g) medium (41/50) raw shrimp, peeled and deveined

½ lb (225 g) fried tofu puffs, halved

1–1¼ cups (240–300 ml) low-sodium chicken stock

¾ cup (180 ml) Air Asam (page 188) or 1¼ cups (300 ml) store-bought tamarind concentrate

3 tablespoons shaved palm sugar or brown sugar

2 tablespoons fish sauce

½ teaspoon fine sea salt

2 cups (180 g) bean sprouts

3 Chinese chives or regular chives, cut into 1-inch (2.5-cm) lengths

Egg Ribbons (page 178)

1 medium-hot finger-length red chili, such Fresno, cayenne, or serrano, seeded (optional) and thinly sliced

4 key limes or 2 Persian limes, halved or cut into wedges

The name of this popular dish in Singapore and Malaysia comes from the old name for Thailand—Siam. In fact, its sweet and sour flavors are reminiscent of pad Thai. I could easily buy mee Siam at my school canteen or at the neighborhood hawker center for breakfast or lunch. There are two versions of mee Siam—one with broth, and one that's dry. Julia makes the brothy version, while I like to make the dry version and it's the recipe I offer you here.

Soak the vermicelli in warm water for about 10 minutes or until they soften. Drain and set aside.

To make the spice paste, pulse the shallots, garlic, chopped chilies, dried shrimp (if using), yellow bean sauce, and terasi bakar with 1 tablespoon of oil in a small food processor or blender until the texture of oatmeal, about 1 minute. Scrape down the sides of the bowl as necessary. Or use a mortar and pestle (add the ingredients one by one with a pinch of salt.)

Heat the remaining 2 tablespoons of oil in a wok or large, heavy skillet over medium heat until shimmering hot. Add the spice paste and stir and cook until it is very fragrant and has turned a few shades darker (this indicates the shallots are caramelizing), 5–7 minutes. Reduce the heat if the paste is browning too fast; you don't want the paste to burn. Once the moisture has evaporated, the ingredients will separate from the oil. The paste is now ready for the next step.

Add the shrimp and tofu and stir and cook until the shrimp just turn pink, 1–2 minutes. Add 1 cup (240 ml) of stock, the air asam, sugar, fish sauce, and salt. Raise the heat to medium-high. Add the vermicelli and stir and cook until the strands are well coated and tender to the bite and all the liquid has been absorbed, 2–3 minutes. If the vermicelli is still hard, add the remaining ¼ cup (60 ml) of stock, a little at a time, and continue to cook. Add the bean sprouts and chives. Stir and cook until the vegetables wilt, about 1 minute. Taste and adjust the seasonings if desired. It should have a nice balance of sweet, sour, and spicy. (The saltiness of this dish depends on the yellow bean sauce.)

Transfer to a large serving bowl. Garnish with egg ribbons and sliced chili. Serve immediately with the limes.

Coconut Noodle Soup with Chicken

LAKSA AYAM

Makes 4–6 servings

FOR THE CHICKEN

1½ lb (680 g) bone-in, skin-on chicken thighs or breasts

½ teaspoon fine sea salt

FOR THE SPICE PASTE AND SOUP

3 candlenuts or unsalted macadamias

1 tablespoon coriander seeds or ground coriander

6 Asian shallots or 3 European shallots, chopped

3 cloves garlic, smashed

1 tablespoon dried shrimp, soaked in water and patted dry

2 teaspoons ground turmeric

2 tablespoons + 2 teaspoons vegetable oil, divided

2 salam leaves or makrut lime leaves

2 stalks lemongrass, trimmed and bruised

2 (½-inch/12-mm) slices galangal or fresh ginger

1 can (13.5 fl oz/400 ml) unsweetened coconut milk

1½ teaspoons fine sea salt

1 teaspoon sugar

½ teaspoon ground white or black pepper

½ lb (225 g) large (26/35) raw shrimp, peeled and deveined (optional)

You may have tried laksa, but it was probably curry laksa, the spicy coconut noodle soup popular in Singapore and Malaysia. In fact, there are many forms of laksa from all over the Nusantara region: assam laksa (which is sour and spicy), laksa Tangerang (with a broth of chilies and grated coconut), and this version from Jakarta, where Julia spent her formative years. The list of ingredients may look intimidating, but laksa ayam is quite simple to prepare. Once you've gathered all your ingredients, you're on your way to making a flavor-packed, all-in-one meal suitable even for a weekday.

To cook the chicken, place the chicken pieces in a large saucepan and add water to cover by 1 inch (2.5 cm), usually at least 5 cups (1.2 L). Add the salt. Bring to a boil over medium heat, skimming off any foam and scum that rise to the surface. Reduce the heat to maintain a bare simmer and cook, covered, for 15–20 minutes. Insert an instant-read thermometer into the thickest part of the chicken. It should read at least 165°F (74°C). Or pierce with a knife. The juices should run clear. Remove the chicken and set aside. When cool enough to handle, shred the chicken and reserve the light stock.

While the chicken cooks, make the spice paste: Toast the candlenuts and coriander seeds separately in a small, dry skillet over medium heat until fragrant and browned, 5–6 minutes each. Crush the candlenuts with the flat part of a knife's blade. Grind the coriander into a coarse powder with a spice grinder or a mortar and pestle. (If using ground coriander, just add it to the food processor in the next step.)

In a small food processor or blender, pulse the candlenuts, coriander, shallots, garlic, dried shrimp, and turmeric with 2 tablespoons of oil until the texture of oatmeal, about 1 minute. Scrape down the sides of the bowl as necessary. Or use a mortar and pestle. (If using a mortar and pestle, grind the coriander first, then add the rest of the ingredients one by one with a pinch of salt.)

Recipe continues

½ lb (225 g) dried rice
vermicelli, prepared according
to package directions

2 cups (180 g) bean sprouts or
shredded green cabbage

4 large hard-boiled eggs, peeled
and halved lengthwise

Fried shallots for serving

½ cup (15 g) lemon basil leaves,
Thai basil leaves, or mint leaves

Sambal Soto (page 166)
for serving

Kecap manis for serving

To make the soup, heat the remaining 2 teaspoons of oil in a large pot over medium heat until shimmering hot. Add the spice paste, salam leaves, lemongrass, and galangal and stir and cook until the paste is very fragrant and has turned a few shades darker (this indicates the shallots are caramelizing), 5–7 minutes. Reduce the heat if the paste is browning too fast; you don't want the paste to burn. Once the moisture has evaporated, the ingredients will separate from the oil. The paste is now ready for the next step.

Add 5 cups (1.2 L) of reserved chicken stock (top it up with water if necessary). Bring to a gentle boil, then reduce the heat to medium-low. Add the coconut milk, salt, sugar, and white pepper. Simmer, stirring constantly and scooping the liquid up high and pouring it back into the pot, for about 10 minutes to allow the flavors to meld. Don't let it boil or the coconut milk will split.

Taste and adjust the seasonings if desired. Add the shrimp (if using) and cook until they just turn pink, 1–2 minutes. Remove from the heat.

To assemble, divide the ingredients among 4 bowls, layering the rice vermicelli, bean sprouts, and shredded chicken. Pour about 1½ cups (350 ml) of hot soup into each bowl, scooping some shrimp at the same time, and top each serving with 2 egg halves, fried shallots, and lemon basil leaves. Serve with sambal soto and kecap manis.

Jakarta Beef Noodle Soup

SOTO MI BETAWI

Makes 4-6 servings

3 tablespoons vegetable oil, divided, plus more if needed

2 lb (1 kg) boneless crosscut beef shank or brisket, trimmed of fat if desired and cut into 1-inch (2.5-cm) cubes

4 teaspoons fine sea salt, divided

1 teaspoon ground white or black pepper

12 cups (2.8 L) water

4 makrut lime leaves

3 salam leaves or bay leaves

2 stalks lemongrass, trimmed and bruised

4 (½-inch/12-mm) slices galangal

2 (¼-inch/6-mm) slices fresh ginger

1 teaspoon coriander seeds or ground coriander

1 yellow onion, chopped

1 leek, white part only, chopped

1 bunch green onions, chopped, white and green parts separated

3 tablespoons kecap manis

1 teaspoon sugar

Whenever I've had soto mi in Jakarta, it's been a cornucopia of beef parts: tendon, tripe, offal and even cow's trotters. While Julia doesn't make it with all these parts, she does save beef fat or scraps with tendon to add flavor to the soup. She never wastes food! You can add them together with the beef cubes and render the fat. Beef shank is a naturally tough piece of meat. But it is a bargain cut, cheaper than both chuck and short ribs, which can also be used in this recipe. When cooked low and slow in stock, all the tough meat fibers and collagen (the stuff that thickens soup and helps support joint health) begin to break down, infusing the stock with a great deal of flavor and resulting in succulent chunks of beef.

Heat 2 tablespoons of oil in a large stockpot over medium heat until shimmering hot. Add the beef cubes and sprinkle with 2 teaspoons of salt and the white pepper. Sear on all sides until browned, 3-4 minutes. Depending on how much fat is rendered, you may need to add more oil as you cook.

Add the water, lime leaves, salam leaves, lemongrass, galangal, and ginger. Raise the heat to medium-high and bring the soup to a gentle boil, skimming off the foam or scum that rises to the surface, for 10 minutes. Don't let the soup come to a rolling boil.

Meanwhile, toast the coriander seeds in a small, dry skillet over medium heat until fragrant and browned, 5-6 minutes. Grind in a spice grinder into a coarse powder or use a mortar and pestle. (If using ground coriander, just add it in the next step.)

Heat the remaining 1 tablespoon of oil in the same skillet over medium heat. Add the yellow onion, leek, and white parts of the green onions and fry until wilted, 3-4 minutes. Add the ground coriander and stir until fragrant, about 1 minute. Add the mixture to the soup.

Cover and simmer over low heat until the beef is tender, about 2 hours. Remove the aromatics and discard. Add the remaining 2 teaspoons of salt, the kecap manis, and sugar. Taste and adjust the seasonings if desired. It should taste salty. If eating immediately, skim the fat off the surface of the soup. Or refrigerate for a few hours or overnight to allow the fat to solidify and remove.

Recipe continues

½ lb (225 g) dried or 1 lb (450 g) fresh, cooked egg noodles

6 oz (170 g) dried rice noodles, prepared according to package directions

¼ head green cabbage, shredded

4 Roma tomatoes, chopped

½ cup (15 g) Chinese celery leaves or parsley, chopped

Fried shallots for serving

Kecap manis for serving

Sambal Soto (page 166) or sambal oelek for serving

2 Persian limes, cut into wedges

NOTES

To use an electric pressure cooker, cook on sauté while you skim the impurities. Then continue as directed and Pressure Cook on high for 40 minutes. Once the cooking cycle is over, release the pressure naturally.

My family likes to eat soto mi with a mix of egg and rice noodles. But fill up your bowl with only one type of noodle if that's what you prefer!

If using fresh egg noodles, rinse with boiling water and separate the strands. Drain and set aside.

To assemble the bowls, divide the egg and rice noodles, beef, cabbage, and tomatoes among individual bowls. Bring the soup to a rolling boil and pour about 1½ cups (350 ml) of soup over each bowl. Sprinkle with the celery leaves, the reserved green parts of the green onions, and fried shallots. Serve with kecap manis, sambal soto, and the lime wedges.

Mixed Vegetable Salad

GADO GADO

Makes 4 servings as a main meal or 6–8 servings as a side dish

2 yellow gold potatoes

2 heaping cups (170 g) shredded green cabbage

2 cups (180 g) bean sprouts

1 chayote, peeled and diced

¼ lb (115 g) green beans, cut into 2-inch (5-cm) lengths

1 cucumber, cut into half-moons

4 large hard-boiled eggs, quartered

½ lb (225 g) fried tofu or tempeh, cut into 2-inch (5-cm) cubes

Fried shallots for serving

2 batches Sambal Kacang II (page 168)

Kecap manis for serving

Krupuk or veggie chips for serving

NOTES

Once mixed with the sauce, gado gado should be eaten the same day.

Gado gado is one of Julia's go-to dishes when serving a crowd and makes a grand appearance at all her gatherings. You can serve gado gado already tossed with peanut sauce, but when people's tastes and allergies are varied, it's easier to let everyone serve themselves. The list of vegetables in this recipe is only a guideline. Feel free to mix and match whatever vegetables are in season: spinach, butter lettuce, tomatoes, green beans—the sky's the limit. Traditionally, krupuk (page 193) is crushed over gado gado, but the vegetable chips or straws you find at supermarkets make a great vegan substitute. For a more substantial meal, serve with Lontong (page 182).

Bring a large pot of salted water to a boil over high heat. Add the potatoes and cook until fork-tender, 20–25 minutes. Peel and cut into 2-inch (5-cm) cubes and set aside.

Meanwhile, prepare an ice bath. Bring a medium pot of water to a boil over high heat. Blanch the cabbage until translucent and wilted, 1–2 minutes, then transfer to the ice bath. When cool, drain on kitchen towels. Set aside. Repeat this process with the bean sprouts (30 seconds to 1 minute), chayote (2–3 minutes), and green beans (3–4 minutes).

Arrange the blanched vegetables, cucumber, eggs, and tofu on a large platter. Sprinkle with fried shallots and serve with sambal kacang, kecap manis, and krupuk.

To eat, pick and choose an assortment of ingredients to put on your plate. Pass the sambal kacang around the table and spoon over the ingredients just as you would salad dressing (and similarly, don't drown your vegetables!). Crush the krupuk on top, drizzle with kecap manis, and sprinkle more fried shallots, if desired. Toss together and enjoy!

VARIATIONS: While gado gado seems to be the gold standard—and the most well-known outside Indonesia— there are many versions of vegetable and peanut sauce dishes from all over Indonesia.

Ketoprak is a filling dish of carbs, vegetables, and tofu with a sauce similar to that of gado gado.

Rujak pengantin literally means "bridal rujak." Instead of being cooked, this dish features raw greens like salad leaves. The sauce is anchored by dried shrimp (ebi) and the tart tang of vinegar.

Stuffed Vegetables

SIOMAY BANDUNG

Makes 4 servings

1 lb (450 g) firm or extra-firm tofu

2 zucchini

5 round or square dumpling skins (optional)

¼ lb (115 g) ground pork

¼ lb (115 g) raw shrimp, peeled, deveined, and minced

2 Asian shallots or 1 European shallot, minced

1 clove garlic, minced

2 green onions, chopped

2 teaspoons sugar

1 teaspoon fine sea salt

¼ teaspoon ground white or black pepper

2 tablespoons tapioca flour or cornstarch

1 large egg

2 yellow gold potatoes, boiled, peeled, and cut into bite-size pieces

4 large hard-boiled eggs, halved

Sambal Kacang II (page 168) for serving

Kecap manis for serving

Fried shallots for serving

FROM OUR RECIPE TESTERS
"I love the Chinese influence of this dish, which seemed like a dim sum–style food that was easier because there wasn't complicated folding or pleating," says recipe tester Laura McCarthy. "The presentation is also very nice with the zucchini and tofu."

Siomay Bandung originates in the Javanese city of Bandung, hence its name. It is influenced by yong tau foo, a popular Hakka Chinese dish comprising vegetables stuffed with pork and shrimp. You can stuff just about any vegetable—from eggplant and mushrooms to potatoes and cabbage. Julia's favorite is bitter melon, and I've put my own spin on this dish by using zucchini. If there's a shrimp allergy or you simply don't like shrimp, firm whitefish fillet like mackerel, cod, or pollock works just as well.

Pat the tofu block dry with paper towels and cut into 4 rectangles. Then cut each rectangle into 2 triangles. You will have 8 triangles. Trim and cut the zucchini crosswise into 8 rounds, each about 1½–2 inches (4–5 cm) thick. Cover the dumpling skins (if using) with a damp cloth.

Stand a tofu triangle on its side. Use a teaspoon or melon baller to remove a scoop from the side facing up, creating a small pocket. Do the same with the zucchini rounds, scooping the seeds from the top. Be careful not to scoop all the way through. Reserve the "guts" for the filling.

To prepare the filling, mix the pork, shrimp, shallots, garlic, green onions, and zucchini guts (mashed or chopped as necessary) in a large bowl with a wooden spoon until well incorporated. Add the sugar, salt, white pepper, tapioca flour, and egg and mix into a sticky paste.

Hold a tofu triangle in one hand and stuff the pocket with 1 tablespoon of filling. The filling won't fit entirely inside the pocket. Instead, smooth it into a mound on top. Repeat until all the tofu and zucchini pieces are stuffed. Wrap any leftover filling in dumpling skins or shape into balls.

Prepare the steamer using the method on page 201. Lightly oil the steamer tray. Arrange the siomay on the tray so they're not touching.

Reduce the heat to medium and carefully place the steamer rack or plate on top. Steam for 15–20 minutes. Stick a toothpick into the filling. If it comes out dry, the siomay are cooked. Remove from the heat and wait for the steam to subside. Carefully lift the lid away from you and remove the siomay.

Divide the siomay, potatoes, and eggs among 4 plates. Drizzle with sambal kacang and kecap manis, then shower with fried shallots.

In Indonesia, there are several ways food is cooked on the grill—straight up (bakar, in the manner of Ayam Panggang Kecap, page 128), threaded on skewers (sate), and wrapped in banana leaves (pepes).

Sate, or satay spelled the English way, is probably the most famous of all the cooking styles. I have fond memories of childhood barbecues with nary a burger or hot dog in sight. Instead, we had satay—either chicken (Sate Ayam, page 129) or pork (Sate Babi Oma, page 139). It was my job to thread small chicken pieces (and skin!) onto soaked bamboo sticks. Then the grill master, aka my dad, would flip the skewers continuously over glowing charcoal until suitably gosong (charred).

Chapter 4

Let's Grill!
Ayo Panggang!

Pepes is a method of wrapping foods—be they vegetables, meat, or seafood—then steaming and/or grilling. You can turn anything into pepes: mushrooms (pepes jamur), tofu (Pepes Tahu, page 134), shrimp (pepes udang), and the list goes on.

Kecap Manis-Glazed Chicken

AYAM PANGGANG KECAP

Makes 4-6 servings

4 teaspoons fine sea salt, divided

¼ cup (60 ml) + 2 tablespoons fresh key lime juice, divided

1 (3–4 lb/1.4–1.8 kg) chicken, cut into 8–10 parts, or 3 lb (1.4 kg) bone-in leg quarters

1 tablespoon + 2 teaspoons vegetable oil, divided

10 candlenuts or unsalted macadamias

8 Asian shallots or 4 European shallots, coarsely chopped

4 cloves garlic, smashed

2 medium-hot finger-length red chilies, such as Fresno, cayenne, or serrano, seeded (optional) and chopped, or 3 teaspoons sambal oelek

2 teaspoons sugar

1 teaspoon ground white or black pepper

6 makrut lime leaves, spines removed

1½ cups (350 ml) kecap manis

½ cup (120 ml) water

Fried shallots for serving

NOTES
Alternatively, you can broil the chicken in the oven on high following the same directions.

This chicken dish tastes best when grilled over a charcoal fire. There's no mistaking the smoky, charred flavor. When Julia made this dish in Singapore, she used makrut limes (the fruit and leaves) and jeruk limo (nasnaran mandarin). The juice and rind of both limes inject a depth of tropical flavor unrivaled by any other citrus available here, although calamansi comes close.

Sprinkle 2 teaspoons of salt and 2 tablespoons of lime juice over the chicken in a large bowl. Rub the salt and juice into the chicken to "clean" it and remove unwanted smells (according to Julia). Pat dry with paper towels.

To make the spice paste, heat 2 teaspoons of oil in a small, heavy skillet over medium heat until shimmering hot. Add the candlenuts and fry, rolling them around the skillet, until lightly charred on all sides, 8-10 minutes. Smash the candlenuts with the flat part of a knife's blade. In the same skillet, add the remaining 1 tablespoon of oil and fry the shallots and garlic separately until golden and fragrant, 2-3 minutes each. Pulse the candlenuts, shallots, garlic, chilies, remaining salt, the sugar, pepper, and lime leaves in a food processor or blender until the texture of oatmeal (the lime leaves will still be stringy), about 1 minute.

Pour in the kecap manis and remaining ¼ cup (60 ml) of lime juice and pulse a few more times until well blended. Divide the sauce in half, reserving a portion for the drizzling sauce and another for the marinade. Dilute the marinade portion with the water. Add the chicken and marinate for at least 4 hours in the refrigerator, preferably overnight.

Coat the grill grate with oil or cooking spray. Prepare a charcoal grill for a medium-hot fire (you can hold your hand at grill level only 3-4 seconds). Or cover and preheat a gas grill to medium-high heat for 10 minutes.

Drain the chicken, reserving the marinade. Grill the chicken pieces, skin-side up, until about half-cooked, 15-20 minutes. Dip in the reserved marinade and smash the chicken pieces with a pestle or meat pounder so that the marinade seeps into the flesh. Continue cooking, with the skin-side against the fire for a nice crisp finish, until an instant-read thermometer inserted into the thickest part of the chicken reads 165°F (74°C), 10-15 minutes longer. Place cooked pieces on a serving platter, pour over the drizzling sauce, and sprinkle with fried shallots. Serve with steamed rice and a vegetable side dish.

Chicken Satay

SATE AYAM

Makes 6–8 servings as a snack or appetizer

1 teaspoon coriander seeds or ground coriander

4 cloves garlic, smashed

1 teaspoon fine sea salt

½ teaspoon ground white or black pepper

½ cup (120 ml) kecap manis, plus more for serving

¼ cup (60 ml) Sambal Kacang II (page 168) or smooth peanut butter (optional)

2 tablespoons vegetable oil

4 makrut lime leaves

2 lb (1 kg) boneless chicken thighs or breasts, with or without skin, cut into ¾-inch (2-cm) dice

About 30 bamboo skewers, soaked in water for at least 30 minutes

2 Asian shallots or 1 European shallot, chopped

1 large cucumber, chopped

Lontong (page 182, optional) for serving

Sambal Kacang II (page 168) or Sambal Kecap (page 166) for serving

Fried shallots for serving

Bird's eye chilies or Thai chilies, seeded (optional), stemmed, and chopped, for serving

Every time I visited my oma in West Jakarta, I was bound to have sate ayam. There was a street vendor (abang sate) who plied the neighborhood, carrying his wares on a bamboo pole stretched across his shoulders. Once he was hailed, he would set up his accoutrements at the gate in front of the house. I would watch impatiently as he continuously turned the skewers on his portable charcoal grill, the intoxicating smell of the grilling meat tickling my nose. Once the satay was cooked, I would devour multiple sticks in a row. Do you know what I loved more than the vendor's chicken satay? His chicken skin satay. Yes, entire skewers threaded with just chicken skin—it was marvelous!

Julia's satay is just as tasty. She flip-flops between two sauces—Sambal Kecap (page 166) and Sambal Kacang II (page 168). I much prefer sambal kecap. If you're making sambal kacang, you can use it in the marinade, too. If not, use peanut butter or just omit. I also recommend using juicier thigh meat instead of lean chicken breast. In addition, keep the skin on. It chars and crisps over the fire and is oh-so delicious.

Toast the coriander seeds in a small, dry skillet over medium heat until fragrant and browned, 5–6 minutes. Grind into a coarse powder with a spice grinder or mortar and pestle. (If using ground coriander, just add it to the bowl in the next step.)

In a large bowl, mix together the ground coriander, garlic, salt, white pepper, kecap manis, sambal kacang (if using), oil, and lime leaves. Taste and adjust the seasonings if desired. The marinade should taste sweet. Toss the chicken with the marinade to coat. Cover and marinate in the refrigerator for at least 1 hour or up to 24 hours.

Thread 5–6 chicken pieces onto each skewer, packing them together to keep them moist and to prevent the skewers from burning. The meat should cover 4–5 inches (10–13 cm). If you can, try not to leave the sharp points exposed. Save the leftover marinade for basting.

Coat the grill grate with oil or cooking spray. Prepare a charcoal grill for a medium-hot fire (you can hold your hand at grill level only 3–4 seconds). Or cover and preheat a gas grill to medium-high heat for 10 minutes.

Recipe continues

Alternatively, you can broil the satay. Position the rack in the oven so that the skewers sit 3 inches (7.5 cm) from the heat source. Preheat the broiler on high for 10 minutes. Line a baking sheet with aluminum foil and arrange the satay so that the meat is in the middle of the pan and the wooden skewers are sticking out a little. Wrap the end of the skewers in foil to prevent them from burning. Slide the pan into the oven and broil for 3 minutes, until the chicken starts developing a few brown spots. Flip each skewer over and broil for 2–3 minutes longer, until cooked through, testing for doneness as described in the recipe.

Working in batches if needed, arrange the satay on the grate and cook, turning often and occasionally basting with marinade, until cooked through and lightly charred, 5–8 minutes. Test for doneness by touching the chicken with your finger. It should feel firm, not squishy, and the insides should not be pink. Transfer the satay to a serving platter and repeat until all the chicken is cooked.

Arrange the satay on a platter with the shallots, cucumber, and lontong (if using) on the side. Pour sambal kacang or sambal kecap over the satay. (If using sambal kacang, drizzle kecap manis over, too.) Sprinkle with fried shallots and chilies.

Grilled Shrimp in Banana Leaves

PEPES UDANG BAKAR

Makes 4 servings

1 lb (450 g) large (31/35) raw shrimp, peeled and deveined

2 tablespoons fresh lime juice

2 teaspoons coriander seeds or ground coriander

1 cup (140 g) diced yellow onion, divided

1 cup (140 g) diced red bell pepper, divided

1 medium-hot finger-length red chili, such as Fresno, cayenne, or serrano, seeded (optional) and chopped, or 2 teaspoons sambal oelek

2 cloves garlic

½ teaspoon fine sea salt

¼ teaspoon ground white or black pepper

4 large (10 15-inch/25 × 38-cm) and 4 small (8 × 8-inch/ 20 × 20-cm) banana leaf pieces, trimmed and wiped with a damp cloth

1 cup (30 g) lemon basil or Thai basil leaves, roughly torn

Toothpicks or a stapler

NOTES

Alternatively, wrap the shrimp in parchment and aluminum foil. Layer an 8-inch (20-cm) square piece of parchment paper on a 10 × 12-inch (25 × 30-cm) piece of foil. Spread one-quarter of the shrimp mixture in the center, scatter with basil, and cover with more parchment and foil. Crimp and seal the edges to form a parcel. Repeat with the remaining ingredients. Reduce the cooking time to 4–6 minutes.

We love to cook foods in banana leaves! They imbue foods with a delicate grassy flavor and fragrance. Plus, it's an economical and environmentally friendly wrapper, not to mention a brilliant way to cook seafood on the grill. If you're tired of the same ol' same ol' when it comes to cooking shrimp on the grill—i.e., on skewers—try this preparation. It's easy and tasty and makes for a pretty presentation. This recipe also works well with scallops, mussels, and clams.

Toss the shrimp with the lime juice in a large bowl.

Toast the coriander seeds in a small, dry skillet over medium heat until fragrant and browned, 5–6 minutes. Grind into a coarse powder with a spice grinder or a mortar and pestle. (If using ground coriander, just add it to the food processor in the next step.)

Pulse the ground coriander, ½ cup (70 g) of onion, ½ cup (70 g) of bell pepper, the chili, garlic, salt, and white pepper in a food processor or blender until finely chopped but not a paste, 15–20 seconds. Add this mixture to the shrimp, then add the remaining ½ cup (70 g) of onion and ½ cup (70 g) of bell pepper.

Layer a small banana leaf on top of a large leaf, their dull sides facing each other and their ribs parallel to you on a dry work surface. (This doubling up prevents the parcel from tearing.) Spread one-quarter of the shrimp mixture in the center. Scatter some of the lemon basil over the top. Pick up the edge closest to you, fold it over the shrimp, and tuck it under. Fold over again to form a parcel. Trim the sides if desired and secure with 1 or 2 toothpicks or use a stapler. You should have a parcel that is about 10 × 4 inches (25 × 10 cm). Repeat with the remaining banana leaves, shrimp, and most of the basil, reserving a little for garnish.

Coat the grill grate with oil or cooking spray. Prepare a charcoal grill for a medium-hot fire (you can hold your hand at grill level only 3–4 seconds). Or cover and preheat a gas grill to medium-high heat for 10 minutes.

Grill the parcels, covered, for 6–8 minutes, until the outer leaves char in spots. Remove the parcels from the grill and place on serving plates. Cut a slit in the center of the leaves and peel back. Scatter with more lemon basil and serve.

Banana Leaf–Wrapped Tofu Packets

PEPES TAHU

Makes 10 packets

1 package (1 lb/450 g) medium-firm tofu

1 teaspoon coriander seeds or ground coriander

8 Asian shallots or 4 European shallots, chopped

4 cloves garlic, smashed

2–4 medium-hot finger-length red chilies, such as Fresno, cayenne, or serrano, seeded (optional) and chopped, or 3–4 teaspoons sambal oelek

1½ teaspoons fine sea salt

1 teaspoon sugar

½ teaspoon ground white or black pepper

3 tablespoons vegetable oil, divided

2 makrut lime leaves

1 stalk lemongrass, trimmed and bruised

1 red bell pepper, diced

2 green onions, thinly sliced

½ cup (15 g) tightly packed lemon basil, cilantro, or mint leaves, plus more for garnish

2 large eggs

Banana leaves cut into 10 (9-inch/23-cm) squares

Toothpicks or a stapler

This tofu and egg dish has a texture that's firm yet delicate and was a hit with Julia's vegetarian patrons at her restaurant. When making this at home, you can substitute up to half the tofu with oyster mushrooms or minced meat, or use chopped tomatoes instead of bell pepper (drain the juices first). Sweet corn kernels and shredded carrot are a tasty addition, too. For a totally edible package, stuff the tofu mixture into bell peppers and steam or grill!

Wrap the tofu in a non-terry kitchen cloth and wring out most of the liquid. You will have about 2 cups (450 g) crumbled tofu. Place in a large bowl.

To make the spice paste, toast the coriander seeds in a small, dry skillet over medium heat until fragrant and browned, 5–6 minutes. Grind into a coarse powder with a spice grinder or mortar and pestle. (If using ground coriander, just add it to the food processor in the next step.)

In a small food processor or blender, pulse the ground coriander, shallots, garlic, chilies, salt, sugar, and white pepper with 1 tablespoon of oil until the texture of oatmeal, about 1 minute. Scrape down the sides of the bowl as necessary. Or use a mortar and pestle. (If using a mortar and pestle, grind the coriander first, then add the rest of the ingredients one by one with a pinch of salt.)

Heat the remaining 2 tablespoons of oil in a large, heavy skillet over medium heat until shimmering hot. Add the spice paste, lime leaves, and lemongrass and stir and cook until it is very fragrant and has turned a few shades darker (this indicates the shallots are caramelizing), 5–7 minutes. Reduce the heat if the paste is browning too fast; you don't want the paste to burn. Once the moisture has evaporated, the ingredients will separate from the oil. Allow to cool for 5 minutes and remove the lime leaves and lemongrass.

Add the spice paste, bell pepper, and green onions to the tofu. Finely chop some of the lemon basil and add immediately to prevent it from turning brown. Taste and adjust the seasonings if desired. Add the eggs and mix until well incorporated.

Alternatively, you can use aluminum foil cut into 9-inch (23-cm) squares. Lift up the foil on opposite sides to meet in the middle above the tofu mixture. Tightly fold down the foil until it reaches the tofu, then crimp to seal. Fold the sides in and crimp to seal. Be sure to seal the ends snugly so that steam doesn't escape during cooking.

Oma says:
You can also cook pepes tahu in a grill pan on the stove.

Lay a banana leaf on a dry work surface, dull-side up with the ribs parallel to you. Scoop 3 tablespoons of the tofu mixture into the center. Top with 1 or 2 whole lemon basil leaves and roll tightly into a packet that is about 4 × 2 inches (10 × 5 cm). Trim the sides with scissors, if desired. Fold the square corners in toward each other to form a triangle and secure the ends with a toothpick or staple.

Prepare the steamer using the method on page 201.

Arrange the tofu packets on the steamer rack.

Reduce the heat to medium and carefully place the steamer rack or plate on top. Steam for 15–20 minutes. Remove from the heat and wait for the steam to subside. Carefully lift the lid away from you. Open a packet to check for doneness. The tofu should be firm to the touch. If necessary, cover and steam in the residual heat for a few minutes longer.

Then grill or broil the packets on high heat for about 5 minutes until the outer leaves are charred in spots. (Pepes is usually steamed first, but you can skip the steaming and grill or broil them for 10-15 minutes.)

Serve warm or at room temperature with steamed rice and a vegetable side dish.

Grilled Fish Cake Wrapped in Banana Leaves

OTAK OTAK

Makes 6 servings as an appetizer or snack

1 teaspoon coriander seeds or ground coriander

6 Asian shallots or 3 European shallots, chopped, or 3 tablespoons Bumbu Dasar Putih (page 186)

3 cloves garlic, smashed

1 medium-hot finger-length red chili, such as Fresno, cayenne, or serrano, seeded (optional) and chopped, or 2 teaspoons sambal oelek

½ lb (225 g) firm whitefish fillet like Spanish mackerel, tilapia, or barramundi

1 tablespoon sugar

½ teaspoon fine sea salt

¼ teaspoon ground white or black pepper

½ cup (60 g) tapioca flour or cornstarch

⅓ cup (80 ml) unsweetened coconut milk

1 large egg white

1 green onion, chopped

Banana leaves cut into 12 (8 × 4-inch/20 × 10-cm) rectangles

Toothpicks or a stapler

Sambal Kacang I (page 167) for serving

Otak otak is a popular snack throughout Southeast Asia with many variations. However, they are all made with fish mince, tapioca flour, and spices, then wrapped in banana leaves and either grilled or steamed. This version originated on the island of Sumatra before spreading across the archipelago.

Toast the coriander seeds in a small, dry skillet over medium heat until fragrant and browned, 5–6 minutes. Grind into a coarse powder with a spice grinder or a mortar and pestle.

Pulse the shallots, garlic, chili, and fish in a small food processor or blender until a rough paste forms, about 1 minute. Add the ground coriander, sugar, salt, and white pepper and pulse a few more times until well incorporated. Scrape down the sides of the bowl as necessary.

Transfer the paste to a medium bowl and mix in the tapioca flour, coconut milk, egg white, and green onion until a smooth paste forms. The fish paste can be refrigerated for up to 24 hours before wrapping in the leaves.

Place 1 banana leaf rectangle on a dry work surface, dull-side up with the ribs parallel to you. Spread 2 tablespoons of fish paste across the center of the leaf so that it stretches about 1 × 4 inches (2.5 × 10 cm). Take the edge closest to you, fold over the filling, and continue wrapping into a thin packet. Secure the open ends with toothpicks or a stapler. Repeat with the remaining banana leaves and fish paste.

Coat the grill grate with oil or cooking spray. Prepare a charcoal grill for a medium-hot fire (you can hold your hand at grill level only 3–4 seconds). Or cover and preheat a gas grill to medium-high heat for 10 minutes. Grill, flipping halfway through cooking, for about 10 minutes, or until the leaves are charred on both sides and the fish cake is cooked through (you'll have to open one to try).

Alternatively, preheat the broiler on high for 10 minutes, then broil the packets for about 10 minutes, flipping halfway through cooking.

Allow to cool for 5 minutes and serve with sambal kacang. They can be eaten as an appetizer or a snack, or as a full meal with steamed rice and a vegetable side dish.

NOTES
You can also steam the otak otak over boiling water for 10 minutes, until the packets are firm to the touch and the fish is cooked through (see page 201).

Once cooked, otak otak can be refrigerated or frozen for up to 1 month. Reheat them in a preheated pan over low heat for 3–5 minutes if refrigerated or 5–7 minutes if frozen. Or reheat in a steamer or microwave.

Oma's Pork Satay

SATE BABI OMA

*Makes 6–8 servings as a snack
or appetizer*

FOR THE SPICE PASTE

8 candlenuts or unsalted
    macadamias

1 tablespoon coriander seeds
    or ground coriander

6 Asian shallots or 3 European
    shallots, chopped (3 oz)

3 cloves garlic, smashed

2 medium-hot finger-length
    red chilies, such as Fresno,
    serrano, or cayenne, seeded
    (optional) and chopped

2 teaspoons ground turmeric

1 teaspoon ground cumin

3 tablespoons vegetable
    oil, divided

5 makrut lime leaves

3 (½-inch/12-mm)
    slices galangal

3 stalks lemongrass,
    trimmed and bruised

⅔ cup (120 g) shaved palm
    sugar or brown sugar

2 teaspoons fine sea salt

3 tablespoons kecap manis

2 lb (1 kg) pork shoulder or a
    mix of shoulder and belly

About 30 bamboo skewers,
    soaked in water for at least
    30 minutes

Julia's five grandsons love their Oma's sate babi. At barbecues, the boys can be seen with a skewer—or two—in each hand. If you have a Korean-centric Asian market nearby, do as Julia does and buy the pork bulgogi cuts (very thin slices of shoulder or belly), which saves you the trouble of slicing the meat. This satay isn't usually served with a sauce, but you may dip it into Sambal Kecap (page 166) or Sambal Kacang II (page 168) if you'd like.

To make the spice paste, toast the candlenuts and coriander seeds separately in a small, dry skillet over medium heat until fragrant and browned, 5–6 minutes each. Smash the candlenuts with the flat part of a knife's blade. Grind the coriander into a coarse powder with a spice grinder or mortar and pestle. (If using ground coriander, just add it to the food processor in the next step.)

In a small food processor or blender, pulse the candlenuts, coriander, shallots, garlic, chilies, turmeric, and cumin with 1 tablespoon of oil until the texture of oatmeal, about 1 minute. Scrape down the sides of the bowl if necessary. (If using a mortar and pestle, grind the coriander first, then add the rest of the ingredients one by one with a pinch of salt.)

Heat the remaining 2 tablespoons of oil in a large, heavy skillet over medium heat until shimmering hot. Add the spice paste, lime leaves, galangal, and lemongrass and stir and cook until it is very fragrant and has turned a few shades darker (this indicates the shallots are caramelizing), 5–7 minutes. Reduce the heat if the paste is browning too fast; you don't want the paste to burn. Once the moisture has evaporated, the ingredients will separate from the oil. The paste is now ready for the next step.

Add the palm sugar, salt, and kecap manis and stir to mix. Once the sugar has completely dissolved and all the ingredients are well mixed, remove from the heat and set aside to cool. Transfer the marinade to a large bowl.

Cut the pork shoulder into thin strips across the grain. Then cut into ¾ × 1¼-inch (2 × 3-cm) pieces. Add the pork to the marinade and stir to coat. Marinate for at least 1 hour and up to 24 hours. If marinating for longer than 2 hours, transfer to a covered container and refrigerate.

Recipe continues

Instead of pork, you can use lamb or sirloin steak. If you don't have skewers, buy pork bulgogi cuts and simply marinate and grill or broil them as is.

Thread the pork onto the skewers. Repeat until each skewer has 4–5 inches (10–13 cm) of pork threaded onto it. Squish the pork pieces together to protect the skewers from burning. (If you're using bulgogi cuts, thread an entire slice at once, weaving the skewer over and under through the center of the pork about every ⅓ inch/9 mm.)

Coat the grill grate with oil or cooking spray. Prepare a charcoal grill for a medium-hot fire (you can hold your hand at grill level only 3–4 seconds). Or cover and preheat a gas grill to medium-high heat for 10 minutes.

Working in batches if necessary, arrange the satay on the grate and cook, turning occasionally, until the pork is cooked through and has crispy charred edges, 6–8 minutes total. Transfer the satay to a serving platter and repeat until all the pork is cooked.

Alternatively, position the rack in the oven so that the satay will be 3 inches (7.5 cm) from the heat source. Preheat the broiler on high for 10 minutes. Line a rimmed baking sheet with aluminum foil and arrange the satay so that the meat is in the middle of the pan and the wooden skewers are sticking out a little. Wrap the end of the skewers in foil to prevent them from burning. Slide the pan into the oven and broil for 3 minutes, until the pork starts developing a few brown spots. Flip each skewer over and broil for 3–4 minutes longer, until cooked through. Test it by touching the pork with your finger. It should be firm, not squishy.

Serve immediately.

FROM OUR RECIPE TESTERS
"It's pretty much the best-tasting satay that I have had!" says recipe tester Paula Enguidanos. "I really like this dish, and it is really the only pork that I will generally eat!"

In Indonesia, regional variations of satay abound. Pork satay, like Sate Babi Oma (Oma's Pork Satay, page 139), is popular with Chinese Indonesians and on the island of Bali, where the vast majority of the population are followers of Hinduism. Julia's chicken satay (page 129) is a riff on the ubiquitous sate ayam Madura, from the island of Madura, off the coast of Java.

Sate, or satay, is believed to have originated in Indonesia when Middle Eastern traders introduced the kebab during the eighth century. Today, there are so many satay variations. Chicken, beef, lamb, pork, and even rabbit and mushrooms are all fair game. Depending on the region, the meat can be cut into cubes or sliced lengthwise.

Traditionally, satay skewers are made from the spines of coconut leaves (lidi), although bamboo skewers are now quite common. In Yogyakarta, a unique satay called sate klathak is made with goat or mutton pieces threaded onto metal skewers, often made from bicycle spokes! Since metal is a good heat conductor, the meat cooks evenly from the inside.

Sate klathak is typically served with a richly spiced gulai (curry soup). Similarly, sate Padang is accompanied by a thick yellow sauce spiced with turmeric, coriander, galangal, and cumin, among other spices. These are not the only deviations from the usual peanut sauce or kecap manis dip. Sometimes the peanut sauce is mixed with petis (black shrimp paste), whereas sate taichan is served with a simple sambal and a squeeze of lime juice.

FUN FACT:
Sate klathak is seasoned only with salt and when the meat is grilled, the salt crackles and pops, making a noise that to locals sounds like "klathak."

Indonesians don't eat dessert per se. In fact, we're more likely to share a plate of fresh fruit to cleanse our palates after a meal. But we do eat sweets and slurp sweet drinks all hours of the day!

Syrups, jellies, tropical fruit, coconut strips, and crushed ice are just some of the ingredients that go into the wide array of sweet drinks that can be likened to shaved ice desserts in other Asian cultures. An example of such a cold and refreshing treat is Es Teler (page 146). Es Alpukat (page 145) is my take on the traditional avocado drinks that I've enjoyed on my trips back to Indonesia.

Chapter 5

Sweets and Drinks

Kue Kue dan Minuman Manis

Several of the goodies in this chapter fall into the category of kue, or cakes. There are two types of kue. Kue basah (wet cakes)—refer to traditional cakes made from indigenous ingredients like tapioca, glutinous rice, palm sugar, and/or coconut milk, such as Ketan Srikaya (page 162), and Dutch-influenced treats that use butter and milk, like Kue Sus (page 158). The second type is kue kering (dry cakes), which are usually what we think of as cookies. They can be stored for weeks or even months.

Iced Avocado Drink

ES ALPUKAT

Makes 4 servings

⅓ cup (80 ml) espresso diluted with ⅔ cup (160 ml) water, or 1 cup (240 ml) strong brewed coffee, cooled

2 cups (475 ml) whole or 2 percent milk

¼ cup (60 ml) Sirop Pandan (recipe follows)

1 large ripe Hass avocado

Chocolate syrup for serving (optional)

Ice cubes for serving

Ground coffee for serving (optional)

Avocado shakes and smoothies are very popular now, but I remember having avocado dessert drinks served this way: in a tall glass over ice with avocado chunks I could scoop out with a spoon. If you prefer, you can blend it like a milkshake—and add ice cream, of course.

The accompanying Sirop Pandan (pandan syrup) is a rich simple syrup steeped with pandan leaves in a 2:1 sugar-to-water ratio. You can easily adjust amounts according to your needs by using 1 pandan leaf for every 1 cup (200 g) of sugar. The cooled syrup can be bottled and keeps in the refrigerator for up to 2 months. You can use the syrup to sweeten teas and other mixed drinks, too.

Combine the diluted espresso, milk, and sirop pandan in a medium bowl. Using a tablespoon, scoop the avocado flesh in bite-size chunks into the bowl. Refrigerate until ready to serve.

To serve, squirt the chocolate syrup (if using) to coat the insides of 4 tall, clear glasses. Divide the espresso mixture equally among them. Add ice cubes and sprinkle with ground coffee (if using) just before serving.

SIROP PANDAN / PANDAN SYRUP

2 cups (400 g) sugar
1 cup (240 ml) water

2 pandan leaves, knotted

Combine the sugar, water, and pandan leaves in a small saucepan and bring to a boil over medium-high heat. Reduce the heat to low and stir continuously until the sugar dissolves, 8–10 minutes.

Let the syrup cool completely. Remove and discard the pandan leaves and pour the syrup into a jar or bottle. Refrigerate for up to 2 months. Makes 1½ cups (350 ml).

Shaved Ice Dessert with Tropical Fruits

ES TELER

Makes 6–8 servings

4 pieces seedless jackfruit, cut into strips

2 ripe large Hass avocados, pitted, peeled, and cubed

1 package (1 lb/450 g) frozen shredded young coconut, thawed and drained

1 can (15 oz/425 g) fruit cocktail in juice

4 cups (950 ml) whole or 2 percent milk

1 cup attap or toddy palm seeds, cut into bite-size pieces

1 cup (240 ml) sweetened condensed milk (about ½ can)

1 cup (240 ml) Sirop Pandan (page 145), plus more as desired

Crushed ice for serving

Ice cream for serving (optional)

NOTES

Attap or toddy palm seeds are sold canned in syrup at Asian markets. You can also replace them with tapioca pearls for a similar chewiness factor. If you can't find frozen young coconut, macapuno preserved in heavy syrup (popular in Filipino cuisine) is a great substitute. It is sold in jars at Asian markets.

When ripe, jackfruit is yellow and sweet. It can be bought fresh or canned in syrup. Don't confuse the ripe yellow fruit with the unripe jackfruit used in savory dishes like Gudeg (page 101).

Indonesia has an assortment of shaved ice desserts and drinks with names as varied—es campur, es doger—as they are delightful to eat. Es teler is my favorite. A mélange of tropical fruit, it is easy to make and goes down easily, too. I could drink multiple glasses in one go. In Indonesia, you can buy es teler from street vendors, food courts, and even fancy restaurants. It is universally loved! Julia makes es teler at all her parties without fail. A riot would ensue if she didn't!

Combine the jackfruit, avocados, coconut, fruit cocktail, milk, attap seeds, condensed milk, and sirop pandan in a large punch bowl. Just before serving, add the ice. Scoop into tall glasses and serve with a spoon. Top with ice cream (if using).

Pandan Pound Cake

KUE PANDAN

Makes 8 servings

10 pandan leaves, cut into
   1–2 inch (2.5–5 cm) pieces

½ cup (120 ml) unsweetened
   coconut milk

2 tablespoons water

1 cup (200 g) sugar

1 cup (250 g) unsalted
   butter, softened

3 large eggs

2 cups (250 g) cake flour
   (see notes)

NOTES

You can make "cake flour" with
all-purpose flour. Measure 1 level
cup (115 g) of all-purpose flour,
remove 2 tablespoons of the flour,
and then place the remaining
flour in a bowl. Add 2 tablespoons
of cornstarch to the flour. Whisk
together to combine and use as
a substitute for 1 cup (115 g) of
cake flour.

If you prefer cupcakes, line a
12-cup muffin pan and adjust
the bake time to 15–20 minutes.

Pandan chiffon cake was a staple of my childhood and Julia made it often. The delicate crumb and floral, grassy scent and flavor are deeply rooted in my taste memory. I just wish I had the confidence to bake it. To be honest, I'm scared of whisking egg whites to stiff peaks. Plus, I don't own a chiffon cake pan. So I devised a simpler-to-make cake that has the same flavors but is more forgiving. Like the traditional pound cake, it uses no leavening agents. Creaming the sugar and butter and using cake flour helps create lift.

Preheat the oven to 325°F (165°C). Grease a 9 × 5-inch (23 × 13-cm) loaf pan, then line with parchment paper.

Blend the pandan leaves with the coconut milk and water in a blender or food processor until the leaves are chopped up like grass clippings. Strain through a fine-mesh sieve, pressing down on the pulp to squeeze out as much juice as possible. You will have about ⅓ cup (80 ml). Top it up with more coconut milk if necessary.

Cream together the sugar and butter in a large bowl with an electric mixer on medium speed until light and fluffy, about 10 minutes. Beat in the eggs, 1 at a time, mixing well after each addition. Beat in the flour alternately with the coconut-pandan mixture, mixing just until you don't see any more traces of flour. Pour the batter into the prepared pan and spread evenly.

Bake for 50–60 minutes, or until a toothpick inserted into the center of the cake comes out clean. Or use an instant-read thermometer; the center should read between 200°–210°F (95°–99°C).

Run a small knife around the edge of the pan. Allow the cake to cool in the pan for 10 minutes, then invert, peel off the parchment, and cool completely on a wire rack.

Sweet Mung Bean Porridge

BUBUR KACANG HIJAU

Makes 4-6 servings

1 cup (200 g) green mung beans

6 cups (1.4 L) + ¼ cup (60 ml) water, divided

1 (1-inch/2.5-cm) piece fresh ginger, smashed

1 pandan leaf, knotted

⅔ cup (120 g) shaved palm sugar or brown sugar

¼ cup (50 g) granulated sugar, plus more as desired

½–1 cup (120–240 ml) unsweetened coconut milk, plus more for serving

Pinch fine sea salt

1 tablespoon tapioca flour

NOTES

I like to add ¼ cup (40 g) of quinoa for extra nutrition and a chewy bite. Rinse in a colander and add it at the same time as the beans.

Julia made this fragrant sweet porridge often when we were growing up. We had it for breakfast or as an afternoon or late-night snack. I still make bubur kacang hijau to this day and enjoy it as a comforting dessert or breakfast on a chilly day.

Sometimes abbreviated as burjo (short for bubur ijo, as it's called in Javanese), the most basic version is prepared with whole mung beans—their green skins still intact—plus water, sugar, and sometimes tangerine peel for flavoring. However, the version Julia and I make with coconut milk and palm sugar is the standard. If you want to be fancy, serve bubur kacang hijau with ketan hitam (black glutinous rice) or roti bakar (grilled bread), or mixed with durian pulp.

Although usually eaten warm, bubur kacang hijau can be served cold. When I don't have mung beans, I use green lentils or split peas.

Rinse the beans and pick out any stones and grit. Soak in a large bowl with enough water to cover by 2 inches (5 mm) for at least 1 hour, preferably overnight. Drain.

Combine the beans and 6 cups (1.4 L) of water in a medium saucepan and bring to a rolling boil over medium-high heat. Use a large spoon to skim off any scum or foam that rises to the surface.

Reduce the heat to medium-low and add the ginger and pandan leaf. Simmer until the beans start to split open and are soft and tender, about 45 minutes. Add more water if the porridge is getting too thick.

Raise the heat to medium. Add the palm and granulated sugars and stir constantly until they dissolve completely, 4–6 minutes.

Stir in the coconut milk and salt. Cook until heated through, 2–3 minutes. Taste and add more coconut milk or sugar if desired.

In a small bowl, stir together the remaining ¼ cup (60 ml) of water and the tapioca flour to make a slurry. Stir the slurry into the saucepan and mix until the porridge thickens, about 1 minute. Remove from the heat and discard the ginger and pandan leaf.

Spoon into individual bowls and drizzle with more coconut milk if desired. Serve warm.

Oma says:

For a fun summer treat, let the bubur kacang hijau cool, then freeze in ice pop molds or clear ice pop bags.

Herbal Drink with Turmeric, Tamarind, and Ginger

JAMU KUNYIT ASAM JAHE

Makes 4 servings

4 oz (100 g) turmeric roots, scrubbed, peeled if desired and chopped, or 1 tablespoon turmeric powder

2 oz (60 g) fresh ginger, scrubbed, peeled if desired and chopped

3 tablespoons (60 g) seedless "wet" tamarind, or 6 tablespoons lime juice

1 pandan leaf, knotted

5 cups (1.25 L) water, divided

5 tablespoons (120 g) palm sugar or brown sugar, or to taste

Pinch of salt

White sugar (optional)

NOTES

Jamu is usually drunk warm or at room temperature but you can drink it chilled if you'd like. Refrigerate for up to 1 week. The good stuff tends to settle at the bottom, so give the bottle a good shake or stir before pouring into a glass.

It is believed that the skin of roots and rhizomes contain medicinal properties. That's why we leave the peels on, even when making spice pastes, and instead give them a good scrub to remove any dirt. However, it's up to you.

Jamu (or djamu) is a traditional herbal elixir with several hundred years of history. Many Indonesian ibus (mothers and older women) swear by them to boost the immune system, reduce inflammation, and cure minor ailments. One popular belief is that jamu can keep ladies slim and youthful. Of course, this is just native hoo-ha and isn't 100 percent backed by science. There are many different concoctions using roots and rhizomes such as kunyit (turmeric), ginger, lengkuas (galangal), kencur (Kaempferia galanga), and also tamarind and other fruit, leaves, and flowers. In Indonesia, the mbok jamu (jamu lady) would ply her wares at the market or in the neighborhoods. With a large bamboo basket filled with assorted bottles strapped to her back, she would walk from house to house calling out "jamu...jamu..."

I got hooked on jamu when I went back to Indonesia in 2022 and came up with my own concoction. Honestly, I actually like the taste of it, but who doesn't love the prospect of staying slim and youthful?

In a blender, combine the turmeric and ginger roots with 1 cup water and process until smooth. There will still be stringy bits.

In a saucepan over medium-high heat, combine the turmeric-ginger juice, tamarind, and pandan leaf with 4 cups water and bring to a boil. Reduce the heat to low and simmer for 30 minutes, stirring occasionally to break up the tamarind. Add the palm sugar and salt, stirring to dissolve. Taste and add more palm sugar or granulated sugar if desired. Strain through a fine-mesh sieve into a glass, jar, or bottle. Serve warm, at room temperature, or chilled.

Coconut Bread Pudding

PUDING KELAPA MUDA

Makes 6–8 servings

3 large eggs

⅓ cup (70 g) sugar

1 teaspoon vanilla extract

¼ teaspoon fine sea salt

1 cup (240 ml) coconut water

1 cup (240 ml) unsweetened coconut milk

5 cups (½ inch/12 mm) cubed Japanese milk bread or store-bought brioche

1 cup (120 g) frozen young coconut strips, thawed (canned or jarred are fine, too)

¼ cup (40 g) raisins

Handful sliced almonds

NOTES
You can use whole or 2 percent milk instead of coconut water and/or coconut milk.

The original name for this dish, klappertaart, is a combination of Indonesian and Dutch. The word *klapper* refers to *kelapa*, the Indonesian word for coconut, and *taart* means "cake" in Dutch. Some recipes turn out a confection that's more cake-like, but the version I grew up eating is like a bread pudding. Hence, I think calling it a coconut pudding (pudding kelapa muda) is more apt. For the bread cubes, try making the milk bread recipe in Roti Bakso (page 29) minus the filling.

Preheat the oven to 350°F (180°C). Grease an 8-inch (20-cm) square baking pan.

Beat together the eggs, sugar, vanilla, and salt in a large bowl. Add the coconut water and coconut milk. Fold in the bread cubes, followed by the young coconut. Allow the bread to soak up the custard mixture for at least 15 minutes.

Pour the mixture into the prepared pan and sprinkle with the raisins and almonds. Bake for 25–30 minutes, or until the liquid has set and the top is golden brown.

Chewy Tapioca Balls

ONGOL ONGOL

Makes 4–6 servings

1 cup (160 g) shaved palm
sugar or brown sugar

2 tablespoons granulated sugar

1 cup (240 ml) water

¼ cup (60 ml) unsweetened
coconut milk

1 cup (115 g) tapioca flour

1 cup (85 g) finely shredded
coconut (see notes)

Pinch fine sea salt

NOTES
Buy finely shredded coconut
in the frozen section of Asian
markets. Refresh by steaming:
Spread a layer of coconut on
a pie plate and steam, stirring
occasionally, until moist and
fluffy, about 10 minutes. Let
the coconut cool completely
before using. If you can only find
desiccated coconut (also labeled
finely shredded for baking),
rehydrate the same way.

Sweet, chewy, and fun to make, ongol ongol is an easy treat to whip up. It was one of the first recipes Julia learned. She had lots of fun preparing it with her mother. My dad, Rudy, remembers his mother selling ongol ongol at the market during the Japanese occupation of the Dutch East Indies to help make ends meet while his father was interned. He'll never forget the time he played with the hot dough. Some spattered onto his right eyebrow, narrowly missing his eye! He still has a scar to remind him of the incident.

In a small saucepan over medium heat, combine the palm sugar, granulated sugar, water, and coconut milk. Bring to a simmer and cook until the sugars dissolve, stirring, about 5 minutes. Set aside to cool for 15 minutes.

Place the tapioca flour in a wok or large, heavy skillet. Add the cooled syrup gradually, mixing with a wooden spatula to remove big lumps. Turn on the heat to medium and stir constantly for 10–15 minutes, until the mixture turns dark brown and gooey (almost like slime!).

Mix the coconut and salt on a rimmed plate or in a shallow bowl.

Using 2 teaspoons, scoop a bite-size piece of the dough and plop it into the coconut. It will be sticky but that's okay. Roll the dough in the coconut until it no longer sticks to your fingers and shape into a ball. Repeat until all the dough is used up.

Ongol ongol is best eaten on the day it's made.

Black Sticky Rice Cake

BOLU KUKUS KETAN HITAM

Makes 8 servings

1¼ cups (230 g) black glutinous rice

2 teaspoons baking powder

¼ teaspoon fine sea salt

4 large eggs, at room temperature

½ cup (100 g) granulated sugar

¼ cup (40 g) shaved palm sugar or brown sugar

½ cup (120 ml) vegetable oil

½ cup (120 ml) unsweetened coconut milk

1 teaspoon vanilla extract

FOR THE COCONUT GLAZE

2 tablespoons unsweetened coconut milk

½–1 cup (60–115 g) powdered sugar

NOTES
Store the cake in a covered cake dish at room temperature for 1–2 days. After this time, refrigerate for up to 1 week or freeze for up to 3 months.

You can also bake this cake at 350°F (180°C) for 40 minutes, but it comes out drier and with a coarser crumb.

Have you had bubur ketan hitam? This sweet black rice porridge, is made with black glutinous rice (ketan hitam) and coconut milk and usually eaten for breakfast or as a snack. And it's absolutely delicious! I was inspired by a recipe in Eleanor Ford's cookbook *Fire Islands* to recreate my favorite sweet porridge in cake form.

Blend the black rice in a high-speed blender (like a Vitamix) until very fine, 1–2 minutes. Sift the resulting flour to remove the larger rice grains. Discard. Sift the black rice flour, baking powder, and salt into a bowl.

Grease an 8-inch (20-cm) soufflé dish (or any 4-cup/950-ml pan that fits in the steamer) with oil. Line the bottom with parchment paper.

Whisk the eggs and granulated and palm sugars in a large bowl until the mixture is thick and frothy, about 2 minutes. Pour the oil, coconut milk, and vanilla into the egg mixture and mix until just incorporated.

Gently fold one-third of the rice flour mixture into the wet ingredients with a spatula. Repeat twice more until all the flour is used up. Stir until the batter is smooth and velvety, but do not overmix. Pour the batter into the prepared dish.

Prepare the steamer using the method on page 201.

Reduce the heat to medium and place the soufflé dish on the steamer rack. Steam for 40 minutes. Insert a skewer into the center of the cake to test for doneness. If it comes out damp but with no batter sticking to it, the cake is done.

Leave the cake in the steamer and remove from the heat. Allow to rest, covered, for 5 minutes. Remove the cake from the steamer and allow to rest for 10 minutes.

Run a knife around the cake to loosen it from the dish. Hold a large plate over the top of the dish and invert the cake into your hand. Lift off the dish and remove the parchment paper from the cake bottom and discard. Transfer the cake to a cooling rack.

To make the coconut glaze, whisk the coconut milk and powdered sugar together in a small bowl. Start with ½ cup (110 g) of sugar and add more if you'd like it sweeter. Once the sugar dissolves completely, pour the glaze over the cake while it's still warm.

Choux Puffs with Custard Cream

KUE SUS

Makes 20–25 puffs

¾ cup (180 ml) water

⅔ cup (80 g) unsalted butter

1 teaspoon sugar

¼ teaspoon fine sea salt

1 cup (115 g) all-purpose flour

5 eggs

Vla (recipe follows)

Powdered sugar for
serving (optional)

NOTES

To store unfilled cream puffs, wrap
them tightly in plastic and place
in an airtight container; they can
be kept frozen for up to 1 month.
To refresh the puffs, preheat the
oven to 350°F (180°C). Transfer the
frozen puffs to a baking sheet and
reheat until crisp, about 5 minutes.
Let cool to room temperature
before filling.

You might be surprised to see choux pastry in an Indonesian
cookbook. Though choux puffs are originally French, they were
brought to Indonesia by the Dutch. This sweet treat, called soes in
Dutch and kue sus (sus cake) in Indonesian, is filled with vla, Dutch
for "custard cream" (aka pastry cream). Julia spikes her vla with rum,
which is the version I grew up eating. I don't usually have rum at
home, so I add almond extract or make a durian cream instead. Feel
free to add fruit puree or any other flavoring to make it your own.

Position 1 rack in the upper third and 1 rack in the lower third of the
oven. Preheat the oven to 400°F (200°C). Line 2 baking sheets with
parchment paper.

Combine the water and butter in a medium saucepan and bring to a
boil over medium-high heat. Remove from the heat and add the sugar,
salt, and flour and stir with a wooden spoon until no lumps remain.

Return to the stove and stir over low heat until a smooth dough forms
and it pulls away from the sides of the pan, 2–3 minutes.

Scrape the dough into a bowl. Allow to cool for 1 minute, or until an
instant-read thermometer reads 145°F (63°C). Beat the eggs into the
dough, 1 at a time, beating thoroughly after each addition. The final
dough should be glossy, smooth, and thick enough to hold its shape.

Transfer the dough to a pastry bag fitted with a ½-inch (12-mm) round
tip, then pipe tablespoon-size mounds onto the prepared baking sheets,
about 2 inches (5 cm) apart. Or use 2 spoons to drop heaping tablespoons
of dough onto the sheet. During this step, make sure you create tall, not
wide, shapes. This will help create puffs with height that are not flat.

Reduce the oven temperature to 375°F (190°C). Transfer the baking
sheets to the upper and lower racks and bake for 25–30 minutes, or until
puffed and golden brown. Switch the pans between the racks and rotate
from back to front after 15 minutes.

Turn off the oven and allow the puffs to cool inside the oven with the door
propped open for 15 minutes. Allow to cool completely on the baking
sheets before filling. Or refrigerate in an airtight container up to 1 day or
freeze for later (see notes).

NOTES

To make durian vla, whisk in 8 oz (225 g) durian puree after adding the cornstarch in the first step.

Cut the pastry puffs in half across the belly on the horizontal. Fill each puff with about 1½ tablespoons of vla. Shower with powdered sugar (if using).

Filled custard puffs are best consumed on the day they're made.

VLA / CUSTARD CREAM FILLING

3 large egg yolks
⅔ cup (140 g) sugar
2½ cups (600 ml) whole
    or 2 percent milk

½ cup (60 g) cornstarch
1 teaspoon vanilla extract
1 tablespoon rum, brandy, or
    almond extract (optional)

Whisk the egg yolks and sugar in a medium saucepan. Gradually add the milk, whisking constantly, until frothy. Then add the cornstarch a little at a time, followed by the vanilla.

Set the saucepan over medium-high heat, whisking often until the custard starts to thicken, 7–8 minutes. Once it thickens and begins to bubble, continue whisking for 1 minute longer. Reduce the heat to medium if it's starting to burn at the bottom.

Strain the custard through a fine-mesh sieve set over a medium heatproof bowl. Immediately place plastic wrap or buttered parchment paper directly on the surface of the custard to prevent a skin from forming and allow to cool.

When cool, whisk in the rum (if using). Use immediately or refrigerate for up to 4 hours. Makes 2½ cups (600 ml).

Oma says:

Save the leftover egg whites and use them to coat Kroket Kentang with breadcrumbs, instead of using whole eggs (page 27).

Coconut Pancakes

SERABI KUAH

Makes 14–16 pancakes

1¾ cups (250 g) rice flour

¼ cup + 2 teaspoons (50 g) glutinous rice flour, tapioca flour, or cornstarch

¼ cup + 2 teaspoons (37 g) all-purpose flour

2 teaspoons baking powder

½ teaspoon fine sea salt

2 tablespoons sugar

½ cup (120 ml) boiling water

2⅓ cups (550 ml) unsweetened coconut milk

1 cup (85 g) finely grated coconut

Kinca Duren for serving (recipe follows)

NOTES

If you only have a larger (10–12 inch/25–30 cm) pan, make 2–3 circles about 3–4 inches (7.5–10 cm) in diameter instead. Use a well-greased egg cutter for a uniform shape.

Serabi and kinca can be stored in the refrigerator for up to 1 week. Simply reheat the serabi by steaming on medium heat for 2–3 minutes or in the microwave on high for 30 seconds to 1 minute. Reheat kinca on the stove over medium heat until just heated through. Don't boil it on high heat or the coconut milk will separate.

Serabi is a popular street food snack, and this version is eaten with a sweet coconut sauce called kinca. In different parts of Indonesia, you can find serabi topped with a cornucopia of ingredients: grated coconut, coarsely ground peanuts, slices of banana or jackfruit, chocolate sprinkles, or a savory topping like shredded cheese.

Julia makes serabi the traditional way with yeast and leaves the batter outside in the sun (or in a warm oven) to rise. However, I don't really want to wait three hours, so I've created a recipe with baking powder for the added lift and signature holes in the pancake. Serve with kinca flavored with durian, or just plain.

Sift the flours, baking powder, and salt into a large bowl. Stir in the sugar. Pour in the boiling water gradually, mixing as you go. The mixture will be lumpy but that's okay.

Add the coconut milk, a little at a time, whisking until a smooth batter forms. Strain through a fine-mesh sieve to remove any lumps if necessary. Fold in the grated coconut.

Preheat a small, heavy nonstick skillet (I use a 6-inch/15-cm cast-iron pan) over high heat until it's very hot. Reduce the heat to medium. Pour ¼ cup (60 ml) of batter into the pan and cook until bubbles appear on the surface and it's almost dry, 1–3 minutes, depending on the pan you're using. Cover to steam the top until completely dry, 30 seconds to 1 minute longer. Transfer the pancake to a wire rack. Repeat until all the batter is used up. Serve immediately with kinca duren.

KINCA DUREN / DURIAN SAUCE

½–¾ cup (80–120 g) shaved palm sugar or brown sugar

¼ cup (50 g) granulated sugar

1 pandan leaf, knotted

1 cup (240 ml) + 2 tablespoons water, divided

6 oz (170 g) seedless durian pulp, mashed

1 cup (240 ml) unsweetened coconut milk

¼ teaspoon fine sea salt

2 teaspoons tapioca flour or cornstarch

Combine ½ cup (80 g) of palm sugar, the granulated sugar, pandan leaf, and 1 cup (240 ml) of water in a medium saucepan over medium heat. Bring to a simmer and cook, stirring, until the sugars dissolve, about 5 minutes.

Add the durian, coconut milk, and salt, stirring and rubbing the durian flesh against the sides of the pot with a wooden spoon to help it disintegrate. Bring to a gentle boil.

Reduce the heat to low and simmer until the mixture thickens, turns cappuccino brown, and the durian disintegrates, 30–45 minutes. Stir occasionally to prevent the bottom from burning. Taste and add more of the palm sugar if desired. Remove the pandan leaf.

In a small bowl, combine the tapioca flour and remaining 2 tablespoons of water to create a slurry. Add the slurry and stir until the sauce thickens some more and coats the back of your spoon.

Serve with serabi or steamed glutinous rice, or spread on toast. Makes 1½ cups (350 ml).

VARIATION: If you're not a fan of durian, you can make this sauce with an equal amount of bananas, soursop, or jackfruit, or just omit the fruit entirely for a simple coconut sauce.

Sweet Rice and Pandan Custard Cake

KETAN SRIKAYA

Makes 8 servings

FOR THE RICE LAYER

2 cups (400 g) glutinous rice

Vegetable oil for greasing

⅔ cup (160 ml) unsweetened coconut milk

1 tablespoon sugar

½ teaspoon fine sea salt

1 pandan leaf, knotted

FOR THE CUSTARD

10 pandan leaves, cut into 1-inch (2.5-cm) pieces, or 3 drops pandan essence

½ cup (120 ml) water

1⅔ cups (385 ml) unsweetened coconut milk, plus more if necessary

4 large eggs

½ cup + 2 tablespoons (125 g) sugar

½ teaspoon fine sea salt

6 tablespoons all-purpose flour or rice flour

3 tablespoons tapioca flour or cornstarch

Drop pandan essence or green food coloring (optional)

Also called seri muka (pretty face) or puteri (princess) salat in Malay, this steamed layered cake is popular throughout the Nusantara region of Indonesia, Singapore, and Malaysia. The bottom is made from ketan, or glutinous rice, and the top layer is a coconut milk and pandan custard. The cake's poetic names are meant to reflect the smooth, satiny finish of the top layer. Once sliced, each piece should have equal parts white rice and green custard. However, as they say, perfection is fleeting. Regardless, the cake will taste lovely!

To make the rice layer, soak the rice in a large bowl with enough water to cover by 2 inches (5 cm) for at least 4 hours or up to 24 hours. Tip the rice into a fine-mesh sieve over another large bowl, shaking to remove excess water, and drain until it stops dripping. Spread the rice out in a 9-inch (23-cm) cake pan, pie plate, or rimmed platter, or the largest size that will fit in your steamer.

Prepare the steamer using the method on page 201.

Reduce the heat to medium and carefully place the cake pan with the drained rice on top of the rack. Steam for 20 minutes. Remove from the heat and wait for the steam to subside. Carefully lift the lid away from you and remove the rice.

While the rice is steaming, combine the coconut milk, sugar, salt, and pandan leaf in a small saucepan, and simmer over medium heat for about 10 minutes. Do not let it come to a rolling boil.

Remove the pandan leaf and pour the sweetened coconut milk over the half-cooked rice. Stir until completely absorbed. (If using a platter, mix the rice with the coconut milk in the saucepan.) Return the rice to the steamer for 20 minutes longer. Remove from the heat and wait for the steam to subside. Carefully lift the lid away from you and test the rice. The rice is cooked when it's translucent and soft. If it seems dry, sprinkle 1–2 tablespoons of water over the rice and cover for a few minutes to allow it to steam in the residual heat. Once ready, remove from the heat, crack the cover open, and set aside until cool enough to handle.

I use an 8-inch (20-cm) square pan because that's what I have at home. Use whatever you have: A 9-inch (23-cm) round pan or 9 × 5-inch (23 × 13-cm) loaf pan will also work. Just make sure the pan fits into your steamer and adjust the steaming time if necessary.

Depending on your preference, you can cook the rice layer longer for a softer texture.

Once completely cooled, store the cake in an airtight container at room temperature and consume within 24 hours. Do not refrigerate; the glutinous rice will harden.

Grease an 8-inch (20-cm) square pan with oil, including the sides. Line just the bottom with a square piece of parchment paper or banana leaf.

Press the cooked rice firmly into the bottom of the prepared pan. Use a flat tool (like a bench scraper) to tamp down and create an even, compact layer. Prick lightly with a fork all over so that the custard layer will adhere to the rice better.

To make the custard, blend the pandan leaves with the water in a blender until finely chopped like grass clippings, about 30 seconds. Strain through a fine-mesh sieve and press out as much juice as possible. You should get about ⅓ cup (80 ml) of juice. Combine with the coconut milk, adding more (or less) coconut milk if necessary to yield 2 cups (475 ml) of liquid.

Stir together the eggs, sugar, and salt in a large bowl (preferably with a spout) until the sugar dissolves. Stir in the coconut-pandan mixture. Then gradually stir in the all-purpose flour and tapioca flour until well combined. There will be lumps. Mix in the pandan essence (if using).

Hold a fine-mesh sieve over the pan and pour the custard slowly and evenly over the rice, pushing the lumps through with a spoon. Tap the sides of the pan to remove air bubbles and prick any remaining bubbles with a toothpick to create a smooth surface. Cover tightly with aluminum foil.

Prepare the steamer and steam on low with the cover ajar for 40 minutes, or until the custard doesn't jiggle anymore. Insert a toothpick into the center. If it comes out damp but clean, the cake is done.

Cool completely on a wire rack, about 4 hours. Run a knife (rub the blade with oil to prevent sticking) around the edge of the pan to loosen the cake, then cut into slices, diamonds, or rectangles and serve.

VARIATION: To make a palm sugar custard instead of pandan, omit the pandan leaves. In a saucepan on the stove top, dissolve ¾ cup (120 g) of shaved palm sugar and ¼ cup (50 g) of granulated sugar in 1 cup (240 ml) of water. Simmer until it reduces to about ½ cup (120 ml). Let cool, add 1 teaspoon of vanilla extract, and continue with the recipe.

Sambal, or sambel in Javanese, is a spicy relish or condiment that centers chilies as the main ingredient. Sambal usually accompanies a meal, whether it's rice, noodles, or soup. Julia can't eat a meal without sambal to dollop on her food!

Chapter 6

Sambals and Pickles

Sambal dan Acar

At her last count, Indonesian food scholar Prof. Dr. Ir. Murdijati Gardjito, reported 352 different types of sambals. That's a lot of sambals! Many are the same but different. What do I mean by that? Sambals use many common ingredients—shallots, garlic, chilies—but they have subtle differences. For instance, I'm unsure when to use fresh, boiled, or roasted chilies. So I asked Julia, the sambal pro. She can tell you which sambal goes with what dish and easily rattles off ingredients and methods by rote. Her answer: "It's up to you!" In other words, there isn't a definitive answer. It's all a matter of taste.

Like sambal, pickles also add flavor and texture. Some pickles like Acar Kuning (page 173) can be served as an appetizer or side dish, and it's common to have assorted sambals and pickles at a meal.

Chilies in Sweet Soy Sauce

SAMBAL KECAP

Makes ½ cup (120 ml)

8 red and/or green bird's eye chilies or Thai chilies, chopped

2 Asian shallots or 1 European shallot, sliced

2 cloves garlic, minced

⅓ cup (80 ml) kecap manis

1 tablespoon fresh lime juice

This simple sambal is very versatile. It can accompany Sate Ayam (page 129) or be used as a dipping sauce for fried fish or tofu. The sambal may seem overcrowded with shallots and chilies, but that's how it's meant to be.

Mix the chiles, shallots, garlic, kecap manis, and lime juice together in a small bowl. Taste and add more kecap manis or lime juice if desired.

Chili Paste for Soto

SAMBAL SOTO

Makes ¼ cup (60 ml)

8 medium-hot finger-length red chilies, such as Fresno, cayenne, or serrano

2 bird's eye or Thai chilies

Pinch fine sea salt

1 teaspoon fresh lime juice

This sambal is usually paired with soto like Soto Babat (page 48) and also Laksa Ayam (page 118).

In a small saucepan, combine the chilies with enough water to cover by 1 inch (2.5 cm). Place over medium heat and boil for 8 minutes. Drain then stem and seed them if desired. Pulse the chilies with the salt in a small food processor or blender. Or use a mortar and pestle. Stir in the lime juice. Taste and adjust the seasonings if desired.

VARIATION: Stir together 3 tablespoons of sambal oelek with ¼ teaspoon of salt, 1 teaspoon of fresh lime juice, and 2 tablespoons of water.

SAMBAL MAKING TIPS

· Julia gives you full permission to use a food processor to make sambal (and any of your spice pastes), especially with large quantities. If you're making a small amount, by all means use your mortar and pestle. And if you have neither, chop all the ingredients as finely as possible.

· If making sambal in large quantities, freeze in ice cube trays. This makes it easy to pop out small quantities at a time.

· I discovered that boiling the chilies first will tame their heat. However, if you do end up with sambal that's way too spicy, keep frying until the heat dissipates. You can also add something acidic, like lime juice or vinegar, and some sugar. Both should counteract the spiciness. Another option is to add more ingredients, perhaps shallots, kecap manis, or oil.

Peanut Dipping Sauce

SAMBAL KACANG I

Makes ⅓ cup (80 ml)

1 tablespoon vegetable oil, plus more if needed

1½ oz (40 g) raw peanuts (preferably skin-on like Spanish peanuts) or 2 tablespoons store-bought chunky peanut butter

2 medium-hot finger-length red chilies, such as Fresno, cayenne, or serrano, seeded (optional) and chopped, or 1 tablespoon sambal oelek

2 bird's eye chilies or Thai chilies, stemmed (optional)

1 clove garlic, minced

1 tablespoon shaved palm sugar or brown sugar

¼ teaspoon fine sea salt

3 tablespoons hot water

2 teaspoons distilled white vinegar

1 teaspoon kecap manis (optional)

Oma says:
You can use Air Asam or lime juice instead of vinegar. It's up to you.

A little loose and laced with the extra zing of vinegar, this is the perfect dipping sauce for Otak Otak (page 136). If you can't find raw peanuts, buy roasted ones (preferably unsalted), skip the roasting, and grind them right away. Better yet, if your grocery store has a DIY peanut butter machine, that's the best substitute. Plus, since it's usually in the bulk section, you can purchase however much you'd like. If using peanut butter, whisk it in with the spice paste.

Heat the oil in a wok or large, heavy skillet over medium heat until shimmering hot. Add the peanuts and stir and cook until the skins turn a darker shade of reddish brown and the insides turn golden brown, 4–6 minutes. Toss them continuously so they cook evenly. They burn quickly, so pay attention!

When the peanuts are done, scoop them up with a slotted spoon and leave to cool on a paper towel–lined plate. Remove any burned peanuts; they will taste bitter.

When the peanuts are cool enough to handle, grind them with a small food processor, blender, or mortar and pestle, until the texture of wet sand. (It will be coarser than peanut butter.) You will get about 3 tablespoons.

Add the red chilies and bird's eye chilies (if using) to the same skillet, adding more oil if it's dry. Fry until the chilies turn brown and are a little charred, 2–3 minutes. This step is optional but will give the chilies a smoky flavor.

Pulse the toasted chilies, garlic, palm sugar, and salt in a small food processor or blender until the texture of oatmeal, about 1 minute. Scrape down the sides of the bowl if necessary. Or use a mortar and pestle.

In a bowl, whisk together the spice paste, ground peanuts, hot water, vinegar, and kecap manis (if using) until well incorporated. It should be the consistency of half-and-half. Add more water if it's too thick or more ground peanuts if it's too thin. Taste and adjust the seasonings if desired.

Peanut Gravy

SAMBAL KACANG II

Makes about 1 cup (240 ml)

2 tablespoons vegetable oil

1 heaping cup (140 g) raw peanuts (preferably skin-on like Spanish peanuts) or ½ heaping cup (140 g) smooth peanut butter

2 Asian shallots or 1 European shallot, chopped (optional)

1 clove garlic, crushed

2 medium-hot finger-length red chilies, such as Fresno, cayenne, or serrano, seeded (optional) and chopped, or 1 tablespoon sambal oelek

5 bird's eye chilies or Thai chilies, stemmed (optional)

3 tablespoons shaved palm sugar or brown sugar

1 teaspoon fine sea salt

½ teaspoon Terasi Bakar (optional)

3 makrut lime leaves (optional)

1 tablespoon "wet" tamarind pulp or 3 tablespoons tamarind concentrate or lime juice

1 cup (240 ml) water

2 tablespoons kecap manis (optional)

In Indonesian, peanut sauce can be called sambal, saus, or bumbu kacang. It also varies in consistency and ingredients. Thick and creamy, this one is perfect for Gado Gado (page 123), satays, and Siomay Bandung (page 125). It is thicker than Sambal Kacang I (page 167) and has the consistency of gravy.

Heat the oil in a wok or large, heavy pot over medium heat until shimmering hot. Add the peanuts and stir and cook until the skins turn a darker shade of reddish brown and the insides turn golden brown, 4–6 minutes. Toss them continuously so they cook evenly and don't burn. They burn quickly, so pay attention!

When the peanuts are done, scoop them up with a slotted spoon and leave to cool on a paper towel–lined plate. Remove any burned peanuts; they will taste bitter.

When the peanuts are cool enough to handle, grind them in a large blender or food processor until the texture of wet sand, 3–4 minutes. (It will be coarser than peanut butter.) You will get about 1 cup. Or pulverize them with a mortar and pestle.

Pulse the shallots (if using), garlic, red chilies, bird's eye chilies (if using), palm sugar, salt, and terasi bakar (if using) in a small food processor or blender until the texture of oatmeal, 30 seconds to 1 minute. Scrape down the sides of the bowl as necessary. Or use a mortar and pestle, adding the ingredients one at a time with a pinch of salt.

Combine the lime leaves (if using), tamarind, and water in a medium saucepan. Bring to a boil over medium heat and simmer for about 5 minutes, breaking up the tamarind pulp with a wooden spoon. Remove the lime leaves and any remaining tamarind solids.

Stir in the ground peanuts or peanut butter, spice paste, and kecap manis (if using) and cook until the mixture starts to bubble. Adjust the heat as needed to maintain a simmer and cook until thick and creamy like gravy, 4–6 minutes, stirring often so that the sauce doesn't stick to the bottom of the pan. Add more water if you'd like the sauce looser. Taste and adjust the seasonings if desired, making sure the acidity of the tamarind sings.

The sauce can be made 2–3 days ahead. Keep covered in the fridge. To reheat, add a little water if it's too thick, and warm on the stove top or in the microwave.

Fermented Shrimp and Chili Paste

JULIA'S SAMBAL TERASI

Makes 2½ cups (600 ml)

½ lb (225 g) medium-hot finger-length red chilies, such as Fresno, cayenne, or serrano, seeded (optional) and chopped, or 1 cup (240 ml) sambal oelek

2–10 red bird's eye chilies or Thai chilies, stemmed (optional)

1 small red bell pepper, chopped

4 Asian shallots or 2 European shallots, chopped

2 cloves garlic, smashed

1 teaspoon Terasi Bakar (page 189), 1 teaspoon anchovy paste, or 2 teaspoons fish sauce

5 tablespoons (75 ml) vegetable oil, divided

1 teaspoon fine sea salt, divided

2 tablespoons shaved palm sugar or brown sugar, or to taste

NOTES

Julia uses the bell pepper for sweetness and to tame the spice. Feel free to substitute with tomatoes or, for a fun twist, an in-season fruit, such as strawberries, gooseberries, or plums.

If you would like to make larger quantities, this recipe is easily doubled.

I was an adult before I learned that the sambal terasi I had been eating most of my life was not the typical sambal terasi you'd find in a warung (traditional restaurant) in Indonesia. For one thing, traditional sambal terasi is usually made fresh to order and tends to be fiery hot! Julia's version is technically a blend of sambal terasi and sambal bajak; the latter has a darker red color and is generally milder and sweeter compared to sambal terasi. This makes for a friendlier sambal for people with low tolerance to the spicy kick of chilies—like me. Because I'm a wuss when it comes to spice, I seed half of the chilies and I don't add the bird's eye chilies.

Pulse the finger-length chilies, bird's eye chilies (if using), bell pepper, shallots, garlic, terasi bakar, 1 tablespoon of oil, and ½ teaspoon of salt in a small food processor or blender until the texture of oatmeal, about 1 minute. Scrape down the sides of the bowl as necessary.

Heat the remaining 4 tablespoons (60 ml) of oil in a large, heavy skillet over medium heat until shimmering hot. Add the spice paste, remaining ½ teaspoon of salt, and the palm sugar and cook, stirring frequently. Reduce the heat if the sambal is browning too fast; you don't want it to burn. When the sambal starts to stick to the pan, after 8–10 minutes, stir continuously until it is very fragrant, has turned several shades darker (this indicates the shallots are caramelizing), and reduces to the consistency of jam, 12–15 minutes. Add a little water to "unstick" the sambal, if necessary. Taste and adjust the seasonings if desired.

Cool completely and transfer to a glass container. Seal and refrigerate for up to 2 weeks or freeze for up to 3 months.

Green Chili Sambal

SAMBAL CABE HIJAU

Makes 1 cup (240 ml)

½ lb (225 g) mild finger-length green chilies, such as jalapeño or serrano, seeded (optional) and chopped

6 small Asian shallots or 3 large European shallots

2 green tomatoes or tomatillos

10 green bird's eye chilies or Thai chilies, stemmed (optional)

2 tablespoons vegetable oil

Any 2 of the following herbs: 2 slices galangal or fresh ginger, 1 stalk lemongrass, 4 makrut lime leaves

2 teaspoons sugar

½ teaspoon fine sea salt

Juice of 2 small key limes or calamansi limes

Notice the ten bird's eye chilies in the ingredient list? That's no mistake. This green chili sambal is from Manado, the second-largest city on the island of Sulawesi, where they are known for their super-spicy food. Julia likes to eat this green sambal with Ikan Goreng (page 71). Personally, I prefer it in Ayam Penyet Sambal Cabe Hijau (page 55), and no bird's eye chilies, heh. She usually boils the ingredients, but I like charring them to deepen the flavors and bring out a subtle sweetness. At our outdoor kitchen in Singapore, Julia would spear a chili or shallot (or a block of shrimp paste!) with a skewer and char it directly over an open flame on the stove top. I find that the simplest and fastest way is to broil ingredients in the oven. You can just as easily use a grill pan or skillet.

Preheat the broiler on high for 5 minutes. Arrange the mild chilies, shallots, and tomatoes in a grill pan, leaving enough space between them so they roast and don't steam. Broil until the chilies darken to almost black and blister, and the shallots and tomatoes and are soft, wrinkly, and lightly charred, 6–10 minutes. Flip them halfway to char the other side. When done, the vegetables should be 60–70 percent charred, not totally burned, and the insides should be soft.

Transfer to a cutting board and cover with a bowl. Allow to cool for about 10 minutes. Peel off the charred skin and chop the chilies, shallots, and tomatoes.

In a small food processor or blender, pulse the charred chilies, shallots, and tomatoes with the bird's eye chilies (if using) 3 or 4 times, until coarsely chopped like chunky salsa (not a paste).

Heat the oil in a large, heavy skillet over medium heat until shimmering hot. Fry the chili mixture until fragrant, 5–7 minutes. Add your chosen herbs, the sugar, and salt and stir and cook until the mixture turns a dull green and is fragrant, 10–15 minutes longer. Remove from the heat and add the lime juice. Taste and adjust the seasonings if desired. Discard the herbs before serving.

Mixed Pickles

ACAR CAMPUR

Makes 2 qt (1.9 L)

2 lb (1 kg) seedless cucumbers, such as Kirby or Persian, cut into bite-size pieces

¾ lb (340 g) cauliflower, cut into bite-size florets

¼ lb (115 g) cabbage, cut into 1-inch (2.5-cm) squares

4 Asian shallots or 2 European shallots

2 carrots, peeled and shredded

1 small red or yellow bell pepper, diced

1½ cups (350 ml) distilled white vinegar

¾ cup (180 ml) water

1½ cups (500 g) sugar

2 tablespoons fine sea salt

Julia makes pickles with whatever vegetables she has on hand and you can, too. Old habits are hard to break, and she always makes more than enough to give away to friends and neighbors. And in true Javanese style, she makes them sweet-sweet! You can, of course, reduce the amount of sugar and salt used.

Toss the cucumbers, cauliflower, cabbage, shallots, carrots, and bell pepper together in a large bowl.

Combine the vinegar, water, sugar, and salt in a medium saucepan and bring to a gentle boil over medium heat. Stir until the sugar and salt dissolve completely. Taste and adjust the seasonings if desired. Remove from the heat and allow to cool.

Pour over the vegetables and mix well. Cover and refrigerate for at least 1 hour, preferably 12 hours, before eating. The pickles will keep in the refrigerator for 1 month.

Yellow Turmeric Pickles

ACAR KUNING

Makes about 4 cups (950 ml)

5 seedless cucumbers, such as Kirby or Persian, peeled and cut into matchsticks

3 carrots, peeled and cut into matchsticks

1½ teaspoons fine sea salt, divided

3 candlenuts or unsalted macadamias

8 Asian shallots or 4 European shallots, coarsely chopped

4 cloves garlic

2–4 red bird's eye chilies or Thai chilies, stemmed (optional)

1 stalk lemongrass, trimmed, bruised, and chopped

½ teaspoon ground turmeric

3 tablespoons vegetable oil, divided

2 salam leaves

2 (½-inch/12-mm) slices galangal

½ cup (120 ml) water, plus more as needed

2 tablespoons distilled white vinegar

2 tablespoons sugar

1 cup (60 g) cauliflower florets

¼ cup (35 g) chopped red bell pepper

¼ cup (35 g) chopped green bell pepper

This yellow-tinged, flavor-packed, sweet and sour pickle is delicious on its own, as a condiment, or as a topping for fried fish. In the spirit of Julia's no-waste policy, you can use leftover spice paste from making Ayam Goreng Kuning (page 51) to make these pickles, too.

Place the cucumbers and carrots in a colander and sprinkle with 1 teaspoon of salt. Allow to sit in the sink for 30 minutes to remove excess water. Rinse with cold running water, drain, and set aside.

To make the spice paste, toast the candlenuts in a small, dry skillet over medium heat until fragrant and browned, 5–6 minutes. Crush with the flat part of a knife's blade.

In a small food processor or blender, pulse the candlenuts, shallots, garlic, chilies (if using), lemongrass, and turmeric with 1 tablespoon of oil until the texture of oatmeal, about 1 minute. Scrape down the sides of the bowl as necessary. Or use a mortar and pestle.

Heat the remaining 2 tablespoons of oil in a wok or large, heavy skillet over medium heat until shimmering hot. Add the spice paste, salam leaves, and galangal and stir and cook until it is very fragrant and has turned a few shades darker (this indicates the shallots are caramelizing), 5–7 minutes. Reduce the heat if the paste is browning too fast; you don't want the paste to burn. Once the moisture has evaporated, the ingredients will separate from the oil. The paste is now ready for the next step.

Pour in the water and bring to a boil. Stir in the vinegar, sugar, and remaining ½ teaspoon of salt. Taste and adjust the seasonings if desired. Remove from the heat and allow to cool completely.

When the pickling marinade has cooled, add the cucumbers, carrots, cauliflower, and red and green bell peppers. Toss to coat. Add more water (¼–½ cup/60–120 ml) if there isn't enough marinade to coat the vegetables. Transfer the pickles to an airtight container and refrigerate, covered, for at least 12 hours.

Fish out the salam leaves and galangal. Serve the pickles at room temperature as a condiment or warm over fried fish.

Chapter 7

Rice and Basic Preparations

Nasi dan Bahan Dasar

Rice is one of Indonesia's most important staples, and there are countless ways to prepare it, ranging from a simple boiled/steamed rice to more elaborate preparations like Nasi Kuning (page 178). Julia and I both have rice cookers at home, but not everyone has one. Hence, I offer a simple stovetop method.

This chapter also features preparations for items that may be challenging to find. Even if you can't find kecap manis (or if you're gluten-free), we still want you to be able to make our recipes! You will find spice pastes to prepare in bulk (Bumbu Dasar Putih, page 186) and directions for making fried shallots (Bawang Goreng, page 185) at home.

White Rice

NASI PUTIH

Makes 2–3 servings

1 cup (200 g) jasmine or other polished long-grain rice, rinsed and drained (page 196)

1¼ cups (300 ml) water

NOTES
This recipe uses dry US cups. The measuring cup that comes with your rice cooker is 180 ml, or approximately ¾ of 1 dry US cup.

Cooking rice can be tricky. While I've given a precise amount of water, you will have to experiment with your stash of rice to see what the optimum rice-to-water ratio is. Determining factors include whether you're cooking new crop or old crop rice (it usually says on the bag). New crop rice requires less water than old crop, which is drier. As a general rule, new crop rice uses a one-to-one ratio, while older rice uses 1 cup (200 g) of rice to 1¼ cups (300 ml) of water.

If the rice is too dry, add more water, a few tablespoons at a time. If it's too soggy, decrease the water bit by bit. Another factor is whether you like your rice just tender or soft and sticky (perfect for eating with your hands!). You may have to make a few pots of mediocre rice before you make one that's just right! One cup of uncooked rice (beras) will produce about 3 cups (470 g) of cooked rice.

Place the rice in a medium saucepan. Add the water, swirling the rice with your hands, and let the grains settle evenly at the bottom of the saucepan. Bring to a boil over high heat. The water will be bubbling around the circumference of the saucepan. Reduce the heat to the lowest possible setting and cover with a tight-fitting lid. Simmer until the rice is tender and all the liquid has been absorbed, 16–18 minutes. The rice will look moist, and the contents will still be bubbling.

Remove from the heat and let the rice steam, covered, for 10 minutes longer. Remove the lid and gently fluff the rice with a fork or rice paddle. The rice should not be lumpy and the individual kernels should be separated.

Keep the rice covered until ready to serve. Serve hot.

Fragrant Coconut Rice

NASI UDUK

Makes 6–8 servings

3 cups (600 g) jasmine or other polished long-grain rice, rinsed and drained (page 196)

3 pandan leaves, knotted

1½ teaspoons salt

1 can (13½ fl oz/400 ml) unsweetened coconut milk

NOTES
This recipe uses dry US cups. The measuring cup that comes with your rice cooker is 180 ml, or approximately ¾ of 1 dry US cup.

Nasi uduk refers to a rice dish cooked in coconut milk and spices that is popular in Betawi (Jakarta) cuisine. Some posit that "uduk" is related to the word "aduk," which means "to mix," and hence the other meaning for "nasi uduk"—a complete meal of coconut rice and several sides. I usually use Thai jasmine rice but any long-grain rice, like basmati or Carolina Gold rice, will work.

Place the rice, pandan leaves, and salt in a rice cooker pot or a large saucepan with a tight-fitting lid.

Add the coconut milk and 2 cups (475 ml) of water. Stir to mix well.

If cooking in a rice cooker, press the Cook button. In about 20 minutes, the rice will be done and the Keep Warm button will light up.

If you are cooking on the stove top, bring the ingredients to a gentle boil over medium heat. Reduce the heat to the lowest possible setting and cover with a tight-fitting lid. Simmer until the rice is tender and all the liquid has been absorbed, 16–18 minutes.

In both cases, remove from the heat and let the rice steam, covered, for 10 minutes longer. Remove the lid and fish out the pandan leaves. Gently fluff the rice with a fork or rice paddle. The rice should not be lumpy and the individual kernels should be separated.

Keep the rice covered until ready to serve. Serve hot.

Yellow Celebration Rice

NASI KUNING

Makes 8-10 servings

2½ cups (490 g) jasmine or other polished long-grain rice

½ cup (100 g) glutinous rice

1 tablespoon + 1 teaspoon ground turmeric, divided

10 salam leaves or makrut lime leaves

1 stalk lemongrass, trimmed and bruised

2 pandan leaves, knotted

1 teaspoon fine sea salt

1 can (13½ fl oz/400 ml) unsweetened coconut milk

4 cups (950 ml) water, divided

Egg Ribbons (optional, recipe follows) for serving

EGG RIBBONS

2 large eggs	1 tablespoon vegetable oil
Pinch fine sea salt	

Beat the eggs and salt in a small bowl. Heat the oil in a small skillet over medium heat until shimmering hot. Add the eggs and cook for 2–3 minutes, flipping halfway when the eggs are almost set on top. When cool enough to handle, roll the omelet into a cigar shape and cut crosswise into ribbons ¼-inch (6-mm) thick ribbons.

Makes 1 cup (220 g)

Selamatan (meaning "to give thanks") refers to a community gathering celebrating everything from a baby's birth to a birthday or wedding. More often than not, a platter of golden-hued nasi kuning molded into a tall cone takes pride of place at the center of these special-occasion feasts. This majestic display is called nasi tumpeng.

Over the decades, Julia has single-handedly made nasi tumpeng for birthdays, anniversaries, and holidays like Christmas. She builds the tumpeng on a round bamboo tray decorated with banana leaves and surrounds the base with myriad dishes, such as Rendang Daging (page 67), Ayam Goreng Kuning (page 51), and Sambal Goreng Sayur Udang (page 100). Then she cuts tomatoes and chilies into flowers for decorations. The finished display is nothing short of spectacular.

Place the jasmine and glutinous rice in a large bowl with enough water to cover by 1 inch (2.5 cm). Stir in 1 tablespoon of turmeric and soak for at least 1 hour or up to 3 hours. Drain in a fine-mesh sieve over a bowl.

Combine the salam leaves, lemongrass, pandan leaves, salt, coconut milk, and 1 cup (240 ml) water in a large saucepan and simmer over medium heat for 5 minutes.

To cook on the stove top, add the rice, coconut milk mixture, 3 cups (700 ml) of water, and remaining 1 teaspoon of turmeric to the saucepan. Bring to a gentle boil over medium heat. Reduce the heat to the lowest possible setting and cover with a tight-fitting lid. Simmer until the rice is tender and all the liquid has been absorbed, 16–18 minutes. Remove from the heat and let the rice steam, covered, for 10 minutes longer. Test both the jasmine and glutinous rice grains to make sure they're cooked.

To cook in a rice cooker, combine the rice, coconut milk mixture, 3 cups (700 ml) of water, and remaining 1 teaspoon of turmeric in a rice cooker pot. Insert the pot and press the Cook button. When the rice has finished cooking and the Keep Warm button lights up, allow to stand for 10 minutes.

For both methods, uncover and fish out the salam leaves, lemongrass, and pandan leaves. Gently fluff the rice with a fork or rice paddle.

Keep the rice covered until ready to serve. Garnish with egg ribbons (if using) before serving

Oma says:
If you don't have salam or makrut lime leaves, increase the amount of lemongrass and pandan. You can also experiment with other aromatics like ginger, galangal, or a cinnamon stick.

Spiced Rice with Anchovies

NASI LIWET

Makes 6–8 servings

Vegetable oil for cooking

3 oz (90 g) dried anchovies

¼ teaspoon sugar (optional)

4 small Asian shallots or 2 large European shallots, sliced

2 cloves garlic, sliced

4 (½-inch/12-mm) slices galangal

4 makrut lime leaves

2 salam leaves (optional)

1 stalk lemongrass, trimmed and bruised

2 medium-hot finger-length red chilies, such as Fresno, cayenne, or serrano, seeded (optional) and sliced on the diagonal

1 mild finger-length green chili, such as jalapeño or serrano, seeded (optional) and sliced

6 red bird's eye chilies or Thai chilies, chopped (optional)

3 cups (600 g) jasmine or other polished long-grain rice, rinsed and drained (page 196)

¼ cup (60 ml) unsweetened coconut milk (optional)

3–3¼ cups (700–750 ml) water

1 teaspoon fine sea salt

½ teaspoon ground white or black pepper

I first had this Sundanese rice dish at a restaurant in Jakarta. The rice was served in a cute, covered aluminum pot with a lid and swinging handle, and when I opened the lid, I was delighted to see little fried anchovies scattered on the top of the rice. I mixed everything together with the rice paddle, and the intoxicating aromas of briny, citrusy, and musky swirled into the air. I fell in love immediately.

Heat 1 inch (2.5 cm) of oil in a small, heavy skillet over medium heat until shimmering hot. Drop in an anchovy to test. If it sizzles, the oil is ready. Add the rest of the anchovies to the hot oil and stir and cook until golden brown, 1–2 minutes. Use a wire-mesh strainer or slotted spoon to scoop out the fish and drain on paper towels. Sprinkle with a little sugar (if using).

Add 3 tablespoons of the anchovy oil to a large saucepan and heat over medium heat until shimmering hot. Add the shallots and garlic and stir until fragrant, 30 seconds to 1 minute. Add the galangal, lime leaves, salam leaves (if using), lemongrass, red and green finger-length chilies, and bird's eye chilies (if using). Stir and cook for 1 minute.

Add the rice and stir to coat the grains with the spiced oil. Add the coconut milk (if using), 3 cups (700 ml) water (or 3¼ cups/750 ml if not using coconut milk), the salt, and white pepper and stir to mix. Bring to a gentle boil over medium heat. Reduce the heat to the lowest possible setting and cover with a tight-fitting lid. Simmer until the rice is tender and all the liquid has been absorbed, 16–18 minutes.

Remove from the heat and let stand, covered, for 10 minutes longer. Uncover and fish out the galangal, lime leaves, and salam leaves and gently fluff the rice with a fork or rice paddle. Keep covered until ready to serve. Add the fried anchovies just before serving.

Compressed Rice Cakes

LONTONG

Makes 6–8 servings (6 rolls)

1 cup (200 g) generic
long-grain rice

4 banana leaves, wiped clean

Toothpicks

Lontong is a compressed rice cake usually eaten with peanut sauce dishes, such as Gado Gado (page 123) and Sate Ayam (page 129), and coconut milk soups, such as soto. It is also an important component of Lontong Cap Go Meh (see sidebar). Traditionally, raw rice is poured into banana leaf tubes and boiled. Once cooked, the rice roll is sliced into pucks. This method usually takes four to eight hours to cook and the lontong can last for days. To save on cooking time, and because it's easier to handle, I parcook the rice. In this case, it's preferable to use a generic long-grain rice (think Uncle Ben's or Mahatma), not jasmine or basmati.

Soak the rice in a bowl with enough water to cover by 1 inch (2.5 cm) for 30 minutes. Drain and rinse in a fine-mesh sieve under cold running water several times.

While the rice is soaking, cut the banana leaves into 12 (10 × 12-inch/ 25 × 30-cm) sections. Fill a large stockpot (preferably one that is big enough to hold the rice rolls standing up) with water and bring to a boil over high heat. Remove from the heat. Using tongs, dip the leaves, a few pieces at a time, in the hot water until they darken in color. This softens the leaves and prevents them from breaking. Wipe them dry and set aside.

Place the soaked rice in a saucepan with ⅔ cup (160 ml) of water. Bring to a boil over high heat. Cover, reduce the heat until it's bubbling gently, low to medium-low, and cook until all the water is absorbed, 7–8 minutes. The rice will not be fully cooked. Set aside until it's cool enough to handle, 15–20 minutes.

Layer 2 pieces of banana leaf, with the shiny green-side up (so the leaf's color will transfer onto the exterior of the rice), and place them on a dry work surface, the ribs parallel to your body. Scoop about ½ cup (80 g) of half-cooked rice onto the bottom third of the leaf. Shape the rice into a log 1½–2 inches (4–5 cm) in diameter.

Roll the banana leaves very tightly into a log and secure the ends with toothpicks. Arrange the rice cakes in the stockpot standing up if possible. Pour in enough water until all the rice cakes are completely submerged. Or lay them down in the pot and place a plate on top to keep them submerged.

Bring the pot of water to a rolling boil over high heat and cook for 15 minutes. Reduce the heat, cover, and simmer until the rice cakes are firm to the touch, at least 2 hours. Add more hot water if necessary to keep the rice cakes submerged.

When the rice cakes are done, remove from the pot and drain in a colander. Set aside until they come to room temperature before unwrapping and cutting, preferably the next day.

Serve at room temperature.

LONTONG CAP GO MEH

The tradition of Lontong Cap Go Meh started with Indonesian Peranakans (those of mixed Indonesian and Chinese heritage) to celebrate Cap Go Meh, the fifteenth and last day of Imlek (Lunar New Year). Legend has it that when Admiral Cheng Ho's ship landed on the northern coast of Java in the 1400s, many sailors stayed behind and married local women. Over the years, their offspring, the Peranakans, assimilated and adapted to local customs and traditions. This led to Lontong Cap Go Meh.

As an Indonesian Peranakan, Julia never fails to conclude the new year festivities with Lontong Cap Go Meh. The spread usually includes Sayur Lodeh (page 44) with chayote, tofu, carrot, and cabbage; Opor Ayam Putih (page 56); Sambal Goreng Sayur Udang (page 100) with bamboo shoots; and sambal goreng with gizzards. The meal is topped with krupuk and a sprinkling of ground soybeans (koyah kedelai) and sweetened grated coconut.

When Julia was growing up in Bandung and Jakarta, her family celebrated Cap Go Meh privately at home because of a decree that prohibited the public celebration of Chinese religious and traditional holidays. Her mother, my poh poh, would make Lontong Cap Go Meh and Julia's favorite new year treat, kue keranjang (nian gao, or sticky new year cake).

When my parents moved to Singapore, Julia would host an annual party to celebrate Cap Go Meh with the local Indonesian community. However, only the adults would eat these dishes; the kids didn't like those foods—I definitely didn't! Today, Julia still celebrates Cap Go Meh with my dad in Seattle. Without fail, she'll share a photo of her mini feast on WhatsApp!

Fried Shallots

BAWANG GORENG

Makes 3 cups (170 g)

Vegetable oil for deep-frying

½ lb (225 g) small Asian shallots or large European shallots, thinly sliced

NOTES
Save the shallot oil for cooking sambals and stir-fries and any other dishes that could benefit from the flavor-infused oil.

Store-bought fried shallots are a permanent feature in my pantry. They're the perfect garnish for just about any dish, whether Indonesian or not. In Singapore, Julia always made her own. I remember coming home from school to find sliced shallots sunning on a large bamboo tray in our garden. The heat from the sunshine dried out the shallots so they crisped up nicely upon frying. You can also dry them in the oven on low heat, or skip this step. Tip: smaller shallots have less water than big ones and crisp up faster.

Heat 2 inches (5 cm) of oil in a large, heavy saucepan over medium-high heat until an instant-read thermometer reads 350°F (180°C). Add a sliced shallot to test. If it sizzles, the oil is ready.

Tip one-third to half of the sliced shallots into the pan, making sure they have room to float freely. They will foam and froth at first because of their moisture, but the bubbles should die down as they cook. Stir continuously to ensure they brown evenly and don't burn. They will soften and wilt before turning golden and crispy, 10–12 minutes. The timing depends on how hot the oil is and how thin the slices are. If the shallots start to burn, adjust the heat accordingly. Once they are done, remove with a slotted spoon and drain on paper towels. The limp shreds will eventually crisp up. Bring the oil back up to temperature before cooking the remaining shallots in batches if necessary.

Store in a tightly sealed container at room temperature for up to a 1 month—if they last that long!

Basic White Spice Paste

BUMBU DASAR PUTIH

Makes about ⅔ cup (160 ml)

3 candlenuts or unsalted macadamias

1 tablespoon coriander seeds or ground coriander

16 Asian shallots or 8 European shallots

8 cloves garlic, smashed

1 teaspoon fine sea salt

½ teaspoon ground white or black pepper

¼ cup (60 ml) vegetable oil, divided

NOTES

To make bumbu dasar merah (red spice paste), omit the coriander. Add ½ lb (240 g) medium-hot chilies like Fresno or cayenne, seeded (optional), and/or 1 large tomato, chopped, and 1 teaspoon sugar to the food processor.

To make bumbu dasar kuning (yellow spice paste), add 1 oz (30 g) fresh turmeric, peeled and chopped, or 1 tablespoon of ground turmeric to the food processor.

Bumbu dasar means "basic spice paste," and there are several bumbu dasar named after their colors: red, yellow, black, and orange. This white paste is the most versatile. While some cooks might include more herbs and spices, I like this simplified version that is suitable for many dishes like stir-fried vegetables and fried rice. Substitute one tablespoon of bumbu dasar putih for every two Asian shallots and one garlic clove combination in any recipe in this book. If you know you'll be using up the spice paste over the next day or two, you can skip cooking it. Just seal, refrigerate, and use when you need it. But if storing for longer than three days, I suggest you fry it according to the directions below. This recipe is easily doubled.

Toast the candlenuts and coriander seeds separately in a small, dry skillet over medium heat until fragrant and/or browned 5–6 minutes each. Crush the candlenuts with the flat part of a knife's blade. Grind the coriander into a coarse powder with a spice grinder or a mortar and pestle. (If using ground coriander, just add it to the food processor in the next step.)

In a small food processor or blender, pulse the candlenuts, coriander, shallots, garlic, salt, and white pepper with 2 tablespoons of oil until the texture of oatmeal, about 1 minute. Scrape down the sides of the bowl as necessary. Or use a mortar and pestle. (If using a mortar and pestle, grind the coriander first, then add the rest of the ingredients one by one with a pinch of salt.)

Heat the remaining 2 tablespoons of oil in a large, heavy skillet over medium heat until shimmering hot. Add the spice paste and stir and cook until it is very fragrant and has turned a few shades darker (this indicates the shallots are caramelizing), 5–7 minutes. Reduce the heat if the paste is browning too fast; you don't want the paste to burn. Once the moisture has evaporated, the ingredients will separate from the oil. The paste is ready now. Cool completely and transfer to a glass container. Seal and refrigerate for up to 2 weeks

Sweet Soy Sauce

KECAP MANIS

Makes about ¼ cup (60 ml)

1 tablespoon water

1 tablespoon soy sauce

¼ cup (40 g) shaved palm sugar or brown sugar

Kecap manis is a seasoning and condiment you don't want to be without when cooking and eating Indonesian food.

In a medium microwave-safe bowl, mix together the water, soy sauce, and palm sugar. Microwave on medium for about 30 seconds. Stir until the sugar dissolves. Scale up the ingredients to make a bigger quantity and store in the refrigerator for up to 1 month.

Tamarind Water

AIR ASAM

Makes 2½ cups (600 ml)

8 oz (225 g) seedless wet tamarind (half a package)

2 cups (475 ml) water

1 cup (240 ml) warm water

NOTES
For smaller amounts, combine 1 tablespoon of tamarind pulp and ½ cup (120 ml) of hot water to make ½ cup (120 ml) of tamarind water.

While tamarind concentrate is readily available, I prefer to make my own tamarind "water." Even though the extract is called water, don't expect it to be runny like its namesake. In fact, the liquid is viscous like fruit juice.

In a small pot over medium-high heat, bring the tamarind and 2 cups (475 ml) of water to a boil. Stir with a wooden spoon to release the pulp for about 10 minutes. Remove from the heat and allow to cool.

When the mixture is cool enough, rub the pulp with your fingers. Push the mixture through a fine-mesh sieve with a wooden spoon, pressing down to release as much extract as possible; reserve the pulp. You will have about 1½ cups (350 ml) of tamarind water. Set aside

In a bowl, combine the leftover pulp with the warm water, stir, and push through the sieve again to yield 1 cup (240 ml) of runnier extract. Stir both batches together and discard the solids in the sieve. Use immediately or cool completely and refrigerate in a sealed container (I use a glass jar) for up to 2 weeks.

You can also freeze tamarind water in an ice cube tray: 1 cube equals 2 tablespoons of tamarind water.

Toasted Shrimp Paste

TERASI BAKAR

Makes 8 oz (225 g) toasted shrimp paste

1 block shrimp paste

Toasting (or roasting) terasi (shrimp paste) enhances its umami and mellows its pungent odor. You can roast the whole block at one go or just a few slices at a time. I offer a few methods. Pick the one easiest for you.

———

Cut as many slices, each ¼ inch (6 mm) thick, as you want from the block of shrimp paste. Open your windows and turn the fan on full blast. Do one of the following:

- Toast the slices in a dry skillet over medium heat until the shrimp paste lightens in color and becomes very fragrant, 5–10 minutes, flipping halfway through cooking.

- Wrap in two layers of aluminum foil and broil on high for 12–14 minutes.

- Place in a small microwave-safe bowl, cover with a plate, and microwave on high for about 45 seconds.

When the shrimp paste is a pale brown (compared to when it was untoasted), breaks like a crisp cracker, and crumbles easily, it is done.

To use, crumble the roasted shrimp paste by grinding with a mortar and pestle. Or place in a zip-top bag and pound with a meat pounder. Measure out as much as you need.

Wrap the remainder in several layers of parchment or foil, or place in a zip-top bag, and store in an airtight container for up to 2 weeks.

Our Indonesian Pantry

This is meant to be a practical cookbook. I *want* you to cook from it. That being said, I know some of the ingredients in this book may not be easy to find outside of Indonesia.

Thankfully, ingredients that form the foundation of many Indonesian dishes, such as shallots, garlic, coriander seeds, and palm sugar (as granulated coconut sugar), are readily available at grocery stores. While aromatics and ingredients like salam leaves, galangal, lime leaves, and terasi (fermented shrimp paste) make Indonesian cuisine special and distinct, they may be harder to find. In all my recipes, I try to offer close substitutes that may result in a slightly different flavor profile. Please don't be deterred. You can still make a tasty dish even if you don't have some or most of these specialized ingredients!

If you can only find dried instead of fresh herbs and spices, substitute in this ratio: the dried ingredient should be one-third the weight of fresh. If possible, try not to make more than one substitution per recipe.

Banana Leaves (Daun Pisang)

In Southeast Asia, banana leaves act like aluminum foil, not only protecting sweet and savory foods while grilling or steaming but also imbuing them with a mild grassy fragrance. Banana leaves are most often available frozen.

Partially defrost frozen leaves at room temperature before unfurling. Use scissors to cut off a section and refreeze any unused potions (they'll keep for up to a year). Rinse and then wipe them dry with a paper towel to remove any white residue. Remove the center spine, trim off any brown edges, and cut to the required size. Particularly stiff leaves can be dipped in boiling water or passed over a flame to soften so they won't crack when folding.

Candlenuts (Kemiri)

With a subtle nutty flavor, candlenuts are blended with other spices to add creaminess to a dish. They are mildly toxic when raw, but the toxicity disappears upon cooking. Toast candlenuts over medium heat in a small heavy skillet (I use a cast-iron pan), rolling them around the pan until they are slightly charred but not burned, five to six minutes. This releases their flavor and aroma. Candlenuts can also be roasted in an oven for about fifteen minutes at 350°F (180°C). Roasting removes most of the water content, allowing for longer storage.

Substitute with unsalted macadamias, or just omit. Note: candlenuts are called kukui nuts in Hawaii and used in poke.

Chilies (Cabe, Cabai, Lombok)

Even though chilies are not native to Indonesia, they are a very important component of Indonesian cooking, adding perfume and heat. That being said, the amount of chilies you use is at your discretion and depends on your personal capsaicin-o-meter (capsaicin is the compound that makes chilies hot). The seeds are the most potent part, so remove them if desired. You can always add them back to the dish for more heat later.

I don't wear rubber gloves when working with chilies. I am careful to handle them by the stem and to not wipe my face or rub my eyes. After handling chilies, I also promptly wash my hands thoroughly with soap and warm water. Another trick I learned is to rub my hands on the side of a stainless-steel sink. Apparently, the steel molecules remove the chili molecules from your skin. I advise beginners to use gloves. Refrigerate chilies in a paper bag for up to two weeks, or freeze for up to three months.

Chili Comparison

In Indonesia, there are three common types of chilies—cabe keriting (curly chili), cabe merah besar (big red chili), and cabe rawit (bird's eye chili). This table compares the Scoville Heat Units (SHU), the measurement for "spiciness" or heat, to chilies found in the United States.

Mild (2,000–10,000 SHU)	Hot (15,000–50,000+ SHU)	Spicy Hot (60,000–100,000+ SHU)	Flaming hot (115,000–250,000+ SHU)
red jalapeños	cabe merah besar	cabe keriting	cabe rawit
Fresno	serrano	Thai chili	habanero
Korean chili pepper	cayenne		
	de arbol		

Bird's eye chilies (cabe rawit)

Only 1½ inches (4 cm) long and ⅛ inch (3 mm) in diameter at their widest, these fiery specimens pack a lot of heat into their little bodies. They are used both fresh and dried and are extremely spicy. Immature green chilies turn red when ripe, but depending on maturity may be orange or purple instead. Bird's eye chilies can be eaten at all stages. Substitute Thai chilies if you like.

Chili powder (cabe bubuk)

Julia sometimes uses chili powder (meaning powder made from hot chilies—not to be mistaken for the spice mix used to make Texas chili) to add color to her dishes. She prefers gochugaru, made from Korean red peppers. This brilliant, flaming red powder has a pungent sweet smell.

Finger-length red chilies (cabe merah besar)

Assorted red chilies that range in length from 4-8 inches (10-20 cm) are sold at Asian markets.

Most remain nameless, and the only way to gauge their flavor is to try them. At the grocery store, you might find Fresno, cayenne, or serrano. I use moderately spiced peppers like Fresno and amp up the heat with bird's eye chilies. If you can't find fresh chilies, substitute with 1½ teaspoons sambal oelek per one finger-length chili, or use dried guajillo or pasilla peppers, soaking them for at least ten minutes.

Sambal oelek

Oelek—or ulek—means to grind, and this chili paste can be easily made by grinding fresh red chilies with salt and lime juice or vinegar into a coarse paste. The ready-made version is convenient and available at most grocery stores. Any other type of chili paste—even Calabrian chili paste—may be used as a substitute.

Chinese Celery Leaves (Daun Seledri)

Slimmer and more delicate than regular supermarket celery, Chinese celery is used in Indonesian cooking mostly for its fragrant leaves, in much the same way as parsley and cilantro. They are always available at Asian markets, but feel free to use regular celery leaves or flat-leaf parsley.

Cloves (Cengkeh)
Native to the Maluku Islands, cloves are used in stews and braises. Their subtly sweet scent and flavor make them a key ingredient in kue nastar (pineapple tarts). Most of the cloves grown in Indonesia are used to make Kretek cigarettes.

Coconut, Grated (Kelapa Parut)
In Indonesia, you can purchase freshly grated coconut at the wet market. While fresh is best, I'm not expecting you to buy a coconut and grate it at home (although you can!). I buy frozen grated coconut, defrost it, then steam for ten minutes. In a pinch, desiccated coconut, which is finely shredded, will work. Shredded coconut, sweetened or unsweetened, is not the same.

Coconut Milk (Santen)
Coconut milk is the creamy, sweet liquid pressed from the freshly grated flesh of mature brown coconuts. In Indonesia, it is prepared fresh right before cooking. Use frozen grated or desiccated coconut to replicate this. High-quality coconut milk is available in cans or aseptic boxes (I recommend Chaokoh and Mae Ploy brands). You can also find frozen or powdered coconut milk, but these are not my first choices. Always buy unsweetened coconut milk and not "cream of coconut." Stir the contents of the can before measuring: the richer coconut cream usually rises to the top, leaving thinner milk below. Coconut milk spoils quickly, so use as soon as possible (it only keeps for a day or two in the refrigerator). Or freeze any unused portions and defrost as necessary.

Coconut Water (Air Kelapa)
Coconut water is the clear, mildly sweet liquid swishing inside young green coconuts. It is used in many dishes and is a popular drink on its own.

Don't confuse coconut water with coconut milk. While fresh coconut water is translucent, coconut milk is thick and creamy. Coconut water is available canned and in clear bags in the frozen section. Adjust for added sugars.

Coriander (Ketumbar)
Coriander is the most widely used spice in Indonesia. Small and round, the tan-colored seeds have a floral, orangey-lemony taste. If you have a spice (or clean coffee) grinder—or a mortar and pestle—buy coriander whole and grind when needed. Toast the seeds first in a dry (no oil) heavy skillet (I like cast iron). Once they start to brown and release their aroma, transfer immediately into a bowl. They will continue to toast because of the residual heat. If they stay in the pan for too long, they will burn and turn bitter once off the heat. Toasting draws out more flavor and dries the seeds out, making it easier to grind them into a fine powder.

Crackers (Krupuk)
Krupuk udang (shrimp crackers) made of dried shrimp, tapioca flour, sugar, and salt is my favorite. They are sold as pinkish, flattened, hard disks. When deep-fried, they puff up into a curvy chip three times their original size and become super crunchy. Other types of krupuk include krupuk ikan (fish) and krupuk bawang putih (garlic). There's also a special cracker made with the melinjo nut called emping.

Crackers, like sambal, are an indispensable part of an Indonesian meal. They are crushed over Gado Gado (page 123), or munched on between bites of Nasi Goreng (page 106).

Sun them or oven bake at 200°F (95°C) before deep-frying and they will puff up readily. It's fun to watch them expand in hot oil and crisp up. Then enjoy the snap in your mouth. Kriuk! If you're lazy like me, microwave a few pieces at a time for about twenty seconds.

Cumin (Jinten)

Cumin, which smells a little like caraway, is added to braises and stews to lend a smoky and earthy flavor to dishes like Opor Ayam Putih (page 56). You can toast cumin seeds before using but be watchful as they burn quickly.

Dried Anchovies (Ikan Teri)

Salted, sun-dried anchovies are much loved in Indonesia. They are available in different sizes, and the ones I use are barely an inch long. The fish are fried until crispy, mixed with peanuts and sambal, and eaten as a snack served with Nasi Uduk (page 177) or stirred into Nasi Liwet (page 181). You can buy them in plastic bags at Asian markets.

Fish Sauce (Kecap Ikan)

Fish sauce is used the same way you'd use soy sauce in Chinese cooking. Instead of soybeans, fresh fish (most often anchovies and sometimes other fish and shellfish) is fermented with salt in large earthenware jugs, wooden casks, or vats. A good fish sauce is a clear, golden-red liquid that's slightly oily with a deep, rich flavor. A wide variety of brands are available in Asian markets, but my favorites are Red Boat, Three Crabs, or Squid brand (Vietnamese), and Tiparos (Thai).

Galangal (Lengkuas or Laos)

Galangal has an earthy aroma and pine-like flavor with a faint hint of citrus. It is one ingredient I would go out of my way to buy at an Asian market. Be sure to remove before serving, as it has a hard, chewy texture. Julia likes to leave the skin on and slice galangal into ½-inch (12-mm) pieces before freezing for up to six months. When needed, she simply tosses the slices into the pot. Although ginger is not a one-for-one substitute, feel free to use it but expect a different flavor profile.

Garlic (Bawang Putih)

Paired with shallots, garlic is one of the foundational ingredients for making Indonesian spice pastes.

Finely chopped garlic is used to flavor stir-fries; when deep-fried, it makes a crispy garnish.

Ginger (Jahe)

Ginger has a warm, zesty flavor and fragrance that adds bite to both sweet and savory dishes. In Indonesian cooking, it is used in spice pastes, smashed (in teas), sliced (always against the grain of the sinew running through it), and even juiced. I don't usually peel ginger, but you can use a teaspoon to scrape off the thin, papery skin. Ginger can also be frozen. I leave the peel on and cut the ginger into slices before freezing. Some recipes call for a thumb-size piece, which is about 2 inches (5 cm) long and 1 inch (2.5 cm) in diameter.

Lemon Basil (Daun Kemangi)

Lemon basil offers the familiar notes you would get from basil (mint and a little anise) with a hint of lemony citrus. The leaves of the lemon basil plant are not as wide as those of Thai or Italian basil and are a paler green. Lemon basil is eaten in Lalapan (page 94), makes a great complement to seafood, and is also used as a garnish for soups. Try lemon verbena or lemon balm as substitutes. Thai basil and Italian basil can stand in, too, but the flavor will be different.

Lemongrass (Sereh)

These yellowish-green stalks have stiff, lance-like leaves and add a delicate citrus flavor.

To prep, trim the bottom hard root end and the woody top. Peel off the loose, tough outer layers to expose the tender white core, then bruise the entire length of the stem with a meat pounder, large knife, or heavy glass to release the aroma and oils. Julia cuts the stalk into four segments and freezes them this way before tossing into soups, braises, and rice. You can also tie the stalk into a knot. If fresh is unavailable, use dried lemongrass and place it in a spice bag for easy removal.

Limes (Jeruk Nipis)

There are many different types of limes used in Indonesian cooking to add zing to soups, sauces, and marinades. Lime wedges are also served as a garnish alongside sambal and kecap manis. Unfortunately, most Indonesian varieties are not commercially available outside Southeast Asia. Substitute with Persian limes (the common grocery store variety), key limes, or calamansi.

Lime Leaves (Daun Jeruk Purut)

Called makrut lime leaves in the United States, the double-barrel leaves are glossy and dark green. They lend a citrusy undertone to coconut milk dishes, soups, and braises. When a recipe calls for one leaf, it refers to both lobes. Fresh leaves are available at many Asian markets in the produce section and freeze nicely for up to six months. Don't buy dried leaves if you can help it, as they lack aroma and flavor. The juice and pebbly rind of the aromatic fruit are used in Indonesian cooking as well, but the fruit is hard to find outside Southeast Asia.

Noodles (Mi)

Noodles are a Chinese invention that Indonesians have taken on as their own. Rice, wheat, and egg noodles are available dried, fresh/uncooked, and fresh/cooked. After cooking, rinse the noodles in cold water to stop the cooking and drain. Sprinkle with oil and toss them about to prevent sticking. Fresh, cooked noodles should be rinsed with hot water and detangled before using.

Cellophane noodles (so-un) are made from mung bean starch. Sometimes called glass noodles or bean threads, they are translucent and have a smooth, slippery texture. Soak in hot water or soup—don't boil—until soft and pliable (about ten minutes). Snip them into shorter lengths for use in stir-fries and stuffings. They are commonly sold dried in packages with eight to ten bundles, each ranging from 1.3–2 oz (35–60 g).

Chinese egg noodles (mi telur) are made with egg and wheat flour and come fresh or dried in various widths and diameters. I often freeze fresh, uncooked noodles. Don't thaw them before using or they will turn soggy. Simply boil for a little longer than directed on the package.

Rice vermicelli (bihun), also called maifun in the United States, look very much like cellophane noodles when dry, but they have a starchier texture and become opaque when cooked. Before using, soak the dried noodles in hot water until they're soft (about fifteen minutes), then cook only briefly.

Thin wheat noodles (mi karet) are stringy noodles made with wheat and water. They range in width from about 1/16 inch (2 mm) for soup to 1/8 inch (3 mm) for pan-frying. They are best fresh; look in the refrigerated section for dry, supple noodles dusted with cornstarch to prevent sticking. Dried noodles are also available.

Nutmeg (Pala)

Nutmeg, a native spice, thrives on the Banda Islands and to a lesser extent, Ambon. It imparts subtle heat and nutty flavor to savory dishes like Pastel Panggang (page 114). Ground nutmeg may be the most convenient option, but nutmeg is at its most flavorful and fragrant when freshly ground from seed. Use a nutmeg grater or Microplane to grate the whole nutmeg seed into your dish.

Oil (Minyak)

Traditionally, coconut oil is the most popular oil used in Indonesian cooking because of the abundance of coconuts. However, vegetable oils (canola, corn, peanut, safflower, soybean, and sunflower), with their neutral flavor and high smoke points, are the most practical and economical choices for the average cook. I usually opt for canola oil because it's versatile, low in saturated fat, and contains omega-3 fatty acids. It's also neutral in taste and ideal for wok or high-heat cooking.

Oyster Sauce (Saus Tiram)

Made from oysters, water, and salt, oyster sauce is popular in stir-fries, noodle dishes, and seafood like Udang Masak Saus Tiram (page 72). I like Maekrua, a Thai brand with no MSG, but Lee Kum Kee and Hop Sing Lung are also high-quality brands.

Palm Sugar (Gula Aren/Jawa/Merah)

Palm sugar is indispensable in Indonesian cooking and added to sweet and savory dishes alike. The type I use is a reddish-brown sugar made from the sap of the fruit of the arenga palm. Complex and smoky, its flavor is similar to, but far surpasses, dark brown sugar. It is sold in a distinctive cylindrical package at Asian markets. Use a chef's knife or vegetable peeler to shave off pieces and then finely chop. Or use a box grater. Measuring by weight is the most accurate.

In my opinion, granulated coconut palm sugar (the kind sold at grocery stores) is the best substitute. Thai palm sugar, which is light tan in color and comes in 2-inch (5-cm) disks that are rounded on one side and flat on the other, are also okay. Dark or light brown sugar is sweeter, so you may want to use less.

Pandan Leaves (Daun Pandan)

A member of the screw pine (Pandanaceae) family, pandan has long, grass-like blades that smell sweet and flowery and taste slightly grassy. The leaves are used to flavor both sweet and savory foods. Tie into a knot or bundle before throwing into the pot. Fresh or frozen leaves are found in Asian markets and freeze well for months. I don't like to use pandan extract because of the food coloring and artificial fragrance, but feel free to use it if that's all you can find.

Peanuts (Kacang Tanah)

Peanuts have been grown in Java for over two hundred years, mostly for their oil, which was and still is used for cooking. They're also ground into peanut sauces for Gado Gado (page 123) and satay. Raw, skin-on peanuts are preferred, but if you're not a fan of frying, buy unsalted roasted peanuts.

Rice (Beras/Nasi)

In Indonesia, rice is revered. There are even two names for it: beras for raw rice and nasi for cooked rice. Dozens of varieties are grown all over the archipelago. But the most consumed fall into two categories: polished **long-grain white rice (nasi)** and **glutinous rice (ketan)**.

In the United States, I eat imported Thai jasmine rice (a medium- to long-grain rice), either white or brown (unmilled rice with a chewy texture and mild, nutty flavor). Named for its mild floral aroma similar to the flower, jasmine rice cooks up light and fluffy. Golden Phoenix, Elephant, and Royal Umbrella are recommended brands. However, you may prefer U.S.-grown long-grain rice, like Carolina Gold. For the most part, white and brown rice can be used interchangeably; just vary the amount of water and cooking time.

Thoroughly rinsing rice removes excess starches that can cause the grains to clump together. It also helps clean off any debris. This is what I do: Rinse the rice in a rice cooker pot or heavy-bottomed saucepan that has a tight-fitting lid (preferably glass so you can observe the changes). Fill halfway with cold water. Using your fingers, swish and slosh the rice grains in the water until the water turns cloudy white. Tilt the container over the sink to drain the water out, cupping your free hand

Glutinous rice is available as long grains (sometimes labeled "malagkit") or short grains (labeled "mochigome"). Its mildly sweet flavor is excellent in desserts and snacks. There is also a black variety (ketan hitam) with a sweet, nutty taste. Before cooking glutinous rice, rinse the raw rice well and soak it overnight. along the container's edge to prevent rice from falling out. Repeat two or three more times until the water comes out mostly clear. It's okay if it's still a little cloudy. Drain.

Be careful not to substitute regular rice for glutinous rice, or vice versa. Raw glutinous rice is fat and opaque, while long-grain rice is skinny and translucent. Once cooked, white glutinous rice turns translucent and clumps together, while regular long-grain rice separates. Note that 1 cup (200 g) of raw rice yields about 3 cups (470 g) of cooked rice.

Rice Flour (Tepung Beras/Ketan)

There are two distinct types of rice flours: regular and glutinous. **Rice flour (tepung beras)**, ground from long-grain rice, is used to make rice noodles as well as various desserts. Don't confuse rice flour with glutinous rice flour. They are not interchangeable. **Glutinous rice flour (tepung ketan)** looks like cornstarch. Mochiko—Japanese glutinous rice flour—is widely available.

Salam Leaves (Daun Salam)

A member of the cassia family, the salam tree is native to Indonesia and Malaysia. Its leaves, used fresh in Asia, have a slightly spicy, woodsy scent and impart a subtle je ne sais quoi to soups and braises much the same way bay leaves do in Western cooking. Fresh leaves are not available in the United States, but dried ones are sold in Asian markets in cellophane bags usually labeled "daun salam—Indian bay leaves."

Measuring 3–4 inches (7.5–10 cm), the brittle leaves are a dusty green. Soak in water for five minutes and drain before using. Despite being called Indian bay leaves, salam and bay leaves are not a one-for-one swap. However, I don't think there's any harm in substituting regular bay leaves in the recipes in this book. Where appropriate, I've also listed makrut limes leaves as an alternative.

Sand Ginger (Kencur)

Sand ginger **(Kaempferia galanga, cutchery, or aromatic ginger)** is sometimes mislabeled as "lesser galangal" or simply "ginger." It belongs to the ginger family and is widely cultivated throughout Southeast Asia. In Indonesia, sand ginger is used as both a medicine and a cooking spice, especially in Javanese and Balinese cuisines. I haven't been able to find it fresh in the United States, but it's sometimes available in dried or powdered form. I don't think it has a substitute, so just omit.

Shallots (Bawang Merah)

The shallots grown in Indonesia are small and often grow in clusters of two or three bulbs attached to a single root. Similarly sized shallots measuring 1½ inches (4 cm) long and 1 inch (2.5 cm) wide can be found at Asian markets in the United States. Each bulb weighs about ½ oz (15 g). In contrast, the larger shallots usually sold at grocery stores are typically 2½ inches (6 cm) long and 1½ inches (4 cm) across and weigh about 1 oz (30 g) each. The smaller shallots are milder and sweeter. However, both will work fine in the recipes in this book. Just be sure to use the correct number of shallots. Red pearl onions or red onions are also an okay substitute.

Fried shallots are generously sprinkled over everything from soups to stir-fries, and they add a wonderful crunch and flavor. You can buy them in plastic containers at Asian markets, but they're easy to fry at home (see page 185).

Shrimp Products (Produk Olahan Udang)

Dried shrimp (ebi) add a distinctive fishy scent and flavor to many dishes and should be used sparingly. The salted, sun-dried baby shrimp are ½–1 inch (12 mm–2.5 cm) in size. Choose dried shrimp that are orangey-pink and soak them for about ten minutes to soften. Find dried shrimp in 8-oz (225-g) plastic packets at Asian markets, imported mostly from Thailand and China. Ground dried shrimp can also be found in little jars.

Dried or fermented shrimp paste (terasi or trassi) is made by fermenting tiny shrimp with salt, grinding them into a smooth paste, then shaping into rectangular blocks. Shrimp paste must be toasted (see page 189) first before adding to spice pastes and sauces. Once cooked, its pungent fishy smell transforms into a delicate aroma and flavor that add an unmistakable nuance to many Indonesian dishes.

Shrimp paste is sold in 8-oz (225-g) blocks at Asian markets, sometimes labeled "belachan" (Malay for terasi). They can be used interchangeably. If you're lucky, you may find small packages of already toasted and granulated shrimp paste. It's so much more convenient to use! After opening, wrap tightly in plastic or aluminum foil and/or an airtight container to prevent its smell from permeating other food and store in the refrigerator. Thai shrimp paste (ngapi), which is softer and moister but a little less pungent, is a good substitute. Or use another umami-laden ingredient like fish sauce, anchovies, or miso.

Soy Sauce (Kecap Asin)

"Salty" soy sauce was first brought to Indonesia by the Chinese sometime during the nineteenth century. Made from fermented roasted soybeans and ground wheat, it is used to season Chinese-influenced dishes like Cap Cay (page 93). In this book, I use only regular soy sauce, which is sometimes called light soy sauce or thin soy sauce; but don't confuse it with "lite" soy sauce, which usually means reduced sodium. Pearl River Bridge and Lee Kum Kee make good soy sauces across the board. If you're gluten-free, look for wheat-free tamari.

Sweet Soy Sauce (Kecap Manis)

Kecap manis is Indonesia's favorite condiment, used for flavoring myriad dishes and for drizzling and dipping. While soy sauce is a Chinese import, kecap manis is thought to be a true-blue Indonesian product. Traditionally made from black soybeans and palm sugar, it is a thick, syrupy liquid reminiscent of smoke and honey. Bango is my favorite brand, but ABC brand is cheaper and more widely available. See page 187 for a recipe to make your own.

Tamarind (Asam/Asam Jawa)

With its mellow sweet-tart tang, tamarind is a popular souring agent with flavors that are more complex than lime or lemon. It is used to enhance everything from sauces to soups. Fresh tamarind pods are available, but I use "wet" tamarind. The sticky, coffee-colored pulp, together with seeds, is partially dried and then pressed into semi-pliable rectangular blocks. To make Air Asam (tamarind water), follow the instructions on page 188. Store-bought tamarind concentrate—processed pulp in a jar or round container—is convenient but the quality varies. You may have to use up to three or four times as much; taste as you go. Substitute with lime juice or vinegar, and adjust the sugar if desired.

Tapioca Flour or Starch (Tepung Tapioka)

Made from the tuber tapioca (also called cassava, manioc, and yucca), tapioca flour is similar in appearance to cornstarch (note that cornstarch is known generically as "maizena" in Indonesia); both can be used to thicken sauces and in marinades. Work quickly as tapioca flour thickens at a lower temperature. Julia prefers tapioca flour to cornstarch for many preparations.

Tempeh (Tempe)

Packed with protein and various vitamins and minerals, tempeh is a fermented soy product that is one of the world's most nutritious superfoods. And it's an Indonesian original! Unlike tofu, which is made from soymilk, tempeh is made from the whole bean. Hulled soybeans are inoculated with a mold (ragi) and wrapped in leaves—most often banana—and left to ferment. After a day or two, a compact cake held together by dense cottony mycelium is formed. Nutty and earthy in flavor, tempeh is delicious simply fried or roasted in the oven. Tempeh is available at health food stores and specialty grocery stores, but there's an increasing number of artisan tempeh makers who sell at farmers' markets and online.

Tofu (Tahu)

Along with tempeh, tofu is a very important source of protein for Indonesians. House Foods, Sunrise Soya Foods, and Sun Luck are good tofu brands available in many markets. Tofu usually comes in 12- to 16-oz (340- to 450-g) packages with a single large block, or two smaller blocks, sitting in a water-filled plastic tub (the water keeps the tofu moist). If the tofu is locally made, it is sometimes sold in open containers or buckets.

At some Asian markets, you will find fried tofu or tofu puffs—golden rectangles or cubes of tofu that have been deep-fried. They're usually sold in plastic bags or Styrofoam trays of twelve to eighteen pieces. If you can't find them, I give you frying instructions on page 83.

Turmeric (Kunyit)

Turmeric gives spice pastes and Nasi Kuning (page 178) their gorgeous golden hue and imbues a peppery, musky flavor. The fresh and dried leaves are also used in cooking. The fresh rhizome has brown skin and a rich orange interior with a gingery taste that is lacking in the ground form. However, the recipes in this book call mostly for the ground version because of convenience. Plus, the stains are tough to remove! Look for ground turmeric that is a pure deep yellow or gold.

White Pepper (Lada, Merica)

Indonesian cooks prefer white pepper to black. While they come from the berries of the same plant, white pepper is milder and has different flavor notes than black pepper. Personally, I wouldn't swap them since the taste and intensity are dissimilar, but buy what you can find. Grinding whole peppercorns just before use is ideal, but I swap in ground white pepper for convenience.

Wood Ear Mushrooms (Jamur Kuping)

Wood ear mushrooms are quite neutral in flavor; their appeal lies in the texture, which is firm and almost rubbery, adding contrast to soups and stuffings. Sold dried in plastic packets (sometimes labeled "auricularia"), the delicate crinkly mushroom has a black surface and grayish underside. Before using, soak in warm water for fifteen minutes, then rinse several times and trim the stem where it was attached to the wood of the tree. Cloud ear mushrooms are thicker but can be used as a substitute.

Wrappers (Kulit Pangsit/Lumpia)

Made with any combination of wheat flour, water, egg, and/or oil, these wrappers, or skins, are versatile. They are available in different shapes at Asian markets and many grocery stores. Use square **dumpling wrappers** (kulit pangsit) labeled "wonton" to make Pangsit Goreng (page 19).

Chinese spring roll wrappers (kulit lumpia) are thin, beige, and come in 4- to 8-inch (10- to 20-cm) squares. Though commonly sold frozen, they are sometimes available freshly made in the refrigerated sections of Asian markets. Choose paper-thin, translucent wrappers. Egg roll wrappers, though thicker, will work as well. Do not use Vietnamese rice paper (used to make fresh Vietnamese spring rolls).

Store wrappers in the refrigerator or freezer, but let them come to room temperature before using. While assembling, cover the stack of wrappers with a damp cloth to keep them moist. The wrappers are very delicate and are prone to tearing, so always buy extra!

Techniques and Equipment

There are several prepping and cooking tech-niques commonly used in Indonesian cooking. However, you don't need exotic equipment to be successful, only the minimum of utensils that you might already have in your kitchen.

Stir-Frying

Stir-frying is a Chinese technique that involves tossing bite-size pieces of food in a large cooking vessel over high heat. The key is to keep things moving swiftly around the wok.

Slide your spatula under the ingredients and keep turning and tossing them up and over one another, making sure they all come into contact with the oil, the hot wok, and the seasonings.

The wok is the standard stir-fry tool. Called kuali in Indonesian or wajan in Javanese, the bowl-shape vessel is ideal for stir-frying (as well as deep-frying, making sambals, braising, and more). The wok distributes heat evenly, while sloping sides ensure food falls back inside rather than over the edge. Avoid aluminum or Teflon-coated woks. Instead, go for a heavy cast-iron wok that won't tip easily or a modern carbon steel flat-bottom wok that conducts heat well and accommodates both large and small amounts of food.

To achieve wok-searing action and flavor, always preheat the wok until hot. It's ready when you feel the heat tickling your palm held 2–3 inches (5–7.5 cm) above. Swirl in the oil and wait until it shimmers before starting. Vegetables only require a medium-high heat. But if you are stir-frying meat, turn up the heat so that the meat is seared as soon as it touches the pan, sealing in the juices. If you don't have a wok, a large skillet, sauté pan, or even a Dutch oven works just as well.

Some stir-fry tips:

- Have all your ingredients prepared and cut to similar size so they'll cook evenly.

- To make the cooking process go faster, parcook your ingredients by blanching or microwaving.

- Stir-fry small amounts of food at a time.

- Make sure the food is dry; a wet or soggy ingredient can lower the heat in the wok.

- Spread the stir-fried food out in a large serving platter and serve immediately because ingredients continue to cook even after they're off the heat.

Equipment: wok, large skillet, sauté pan, or Dutch oven; metal spatula or wooden spoon or spatula

Deep-Frying

Deep-frying involves immersing food completely in hot oil, usually 2–3 cups (475–700 ml) or 2 inches (5 cm) in a 14-inch (35-cm) wok. However, be sure to allow space at the top of the wok for the oil to bubble and rise when the food is dropped in.

The key to successful deep-frying is knowing when the oil is at the right temperature. Preheat the oil to an optimum temperature of 350°–375°F (180°–190°C) over high heat. Then reduce or raise it as needed. If the oil isn't hot enough, the food will simply soak up grease without forming the nice crust we look forward to sinking our teeth into. Too hot, and the exterior will brown—and burn!—before the center of the food is cooked.

If you have an instant-read thermometer or even a candy thermometer, use it. You can also plunge a wooden chopstick into the oil. If bubbles gather around it, the oil should be hot enough. You'll also smell the "hot oil" smell. Or test fry a small portion of whatever it is you're cooking or a bread cube—it should bubble gracefully to the surface and sizzle gently. If it just sits there soaking up oil, wait a minute or two.

When the food is done, remove with a wire-mesh strainer or slotted spoon, shaking off any excess oil, then drain on a plate lined with paper towels to soak up the oil or on a wire rack over a pan to allow excess oil to drip down. Battered or breaded foods will often leave rogue bits in the oil. Use a wire-mesh strainer or slotted spoon to remove them from the oil before frying the next batch.

Pick an oil with a high smoke point—I use cold-pressed canola or sunflower, but grapeseed and peanut oils are also options. Julia used corn oil in Singapore. In the interest of economy, oil can be reused, but not more than twice in my opinion, and then only if you are cooking a similarly flavored food. Filter the oil well through several layers of cheesecloth to remove any sediment, store it in a cool, dry place, and reuse within a week or two. You'll know it has gone bad when it starts smoking quickly or if the color darkens.

Properly fried food is not greasy at all. It will have a crisp exterior and a moist, tender interior. So, take some care in getting this technique right.

Some deep-frying tips:

- Start frying when the oil has reached optimum temperature.

- Minimize splatter by gently sliding food into the oil with tongs or chopsticks.

- Fry in batches to avoid overcrowding.

- Turn the food occasionally for even browning.

- Always bring the temperature back up again before frying the next batch.

- Always bring the temperature back up again before frying the next batch.

Alternatively, you can air-fry most fried foods in this book (just not those with a wet batter). You won't get the exact same results, but the food will still be reasonably crispy.

Instead of the standard 350°–375°F (180°–190°C), an air fryer needs to be at 390°–400°F (about 200°C) because circulating hot air is not as intense as hot oil. Brush or spritz the food with oil, then either flip or toss halfway through cooking and coat with oil once more. The air fryer typically requires a longer cooking time, too. Start with the recipe's required time, then continue to check your food and add more time as you go.

Equipment: wok (12–14 inches/30–35 cm), heavy-bottomed pot, or Dutch oven (4 qt/4 L), wire-mesh strainer; slotted spoon; tongs; cooking chopsticks

Steaming

Steaming is a gentle cooking technique that's perfect for showcasing a food's natural flavors. In Indonesia, cakes are more often steamed than baked, such as Ketan Srikaya (page 162).

There are generally two types of steamers: bamboo steamers are used in a wok, and metal steamers come with a bottom vessel to hold water.

A bamboo steamer has a plaited cover to absorb moisture. As the steam circulates, the condensation collecting on the top of the lid is minimized, thus preventing water from dripping onto the food, which can spoil the taste and appearance of the dish. A metal or glass lid should be wrapped with a kitchen towel to absorb any dripping liquid.

If you don't have a dedicated steamer, you can still steam food using a wok or large pot that has a tight-fitting lid and a wire rack. A stockpot with a pasta insert, an asparagus steamer, or an electric pressure cooker on sauté mode works too! You can also experiment with common kitchen implements as follows:

- Set the removable rim of a springform pan or a round cake rack in a deep, wide pan with a lid. Place a pie dish on top.

- Use a collapsible vegetable steaming rack in a deep skillet or wok.

- Crisscross two wooden chopsticks inside a wok and balance a plate of food on the chopsticks.

- Place a trivet or a small upturned bowl in a wok or a large, wide pot. Place a shallow dish or pie plate on top. Pour in enough water to just reach the trivet.

To steam, fill the bottom vessel with a generous amount of water, stopping before the water level reaches the basket or rack, perhaps 3–4 inches (7.5–10 cm). Cover and bring to a rolling boil over high heat. This will take about 10 minutes.

While steaming, monitor the water level. Steam should be constantly escaping from underneath the lid. Reduce the heat to low and peek at the water level. Replenish, if necessary, with boiling water, then raise the heat back up and continue steaming.

Equipment: bamboo or metal steamer, large pot and wire rack, or electric pressure cooker and trivet

Making Bumbu Bumbu—The Mortar and Pestle versus the Food Processor

At the heart of Indonesian cooking lies bumbu bumbu, an assortment of seasonings and spices. There are two types: bumbu basah (literally "wet seasonings" or spice pastes) and bumbu kering (dry seasonings). They are often used in tandem to flavor meats and seafood or to make soups and curries.

More often than not, when we talk about bumbu, we're referring to bumbu basah. Every bumbu basah starts with shallots and garlic as key ingredients. Then chilies, rhizomes (e.g., turmeric), and/or aromatics (e.g., lemongrass) might be added.

Bumbu kering comprise spices like coriander, cumin, and cloves as well as fragrant leaves like salam leaves and makrut lime leaves. I call the combination of salam, lemongrass, and galangal the Holy Trinity of Javanese cooking because Julia uses them for most of her recipes.

Traditionally, spice pastes are made with a mortar and pestle. There's a reason why this is still the preferred method in many Indonesian kitchens. The typical Indonesian mortar is shaped like a saucer and carved from volcanic stone. It is paired with a pestle shaped like a buffalo horn. The proper technique is to grind the food with a backward and forward motion across the stone, with occasional pounding. This act of crushing and grinding slowly massages food together into a fine, creamy paste. The cell structures burst open, releasing essential oils and resulting in deeper flavor. Overall, the paste will have a more satisfying consistency and complex flavor than one made in a food processor. Plus, you have more control over the consistency of your paste.

A food processor chops everything down, tearing apart and breaking down ingredients, but it doesn't necessarily burst cells to release aromatic compounds.

There is a system to grinding ingredients with a mortar and pestle. Grind the hard spices (e.g., coriander) first. Then add the rest of the ingredients one at a time with a pinch of salt to create friction, starting with the toughest (say, lemongrass), then continuing with softer, moisture-rich ones (e.g., garlic and chilies). The last step is to add crumbly or liquid ingredients like tamarind water or fermented shrimp paste.

To be honest, I use a food processor unless I'm only making small amounts. Chef Yudi (Jero Mangku Dalem Suci Gede Yudiawan), a chef I cooked with in Bali, recommends using a small to medium food processor, preferably a 3- or 4-cup (700- or 950-ml) one. Yes, he approves! The Magic Bullet blender also works great. Pulse until a smooth paste resembling cooked oatmeal is formed (not a puree). A few coarse bits here and there are fine—there isn't an Indonesian grandmother looking over your shoulder!

Some tips on using a food processor:

- Press pulse to run the food processor intermittently. You will get more even results and won't bruise herbs or onions, and this avoids overprocessing or liquefying the ingredients. Pulsing also prevents too much air from being introduced into the paste.

- Add a little liquid (oil, coconut milk, or water, depending on the recipe) to keep the mixture turning.

- Don't overload it. Pulse in batches, if necessary.

- If the mixture is sticking to the sides, turn off the machine, shake the bowl, and open. Push the ingredients to the center with a spatula.

Whichever method you choose, it helps to peel and chop all the ingredients first. Even though you can, Julia doesn't usually grind the harder herbs like lemongrass and galangal. In all the recipes, sliced galangal and bruised lemongrass are added when frying the paste. You can fish them out when you're done cooking or leave them in for a more rustic presentation. Just remind your guests not to eat them!

In the end, using a food processor is definitely more efficient, especially if making spice pastes in bulk, but if you have the time and inclination, use a mortar and pestle. It is a very meditative and therapeutic way to connect with your food both physically and spiritually.

Cooking Spice Pastes and Sambals

When cooking spice pastes, you need a good amount of oil to prevent the paste from drying out and burning. Don't skimp and don't be afraid to add more oil if the ingredients look like they're burning. The oil also helps the ingredients caramelize. Once the moisture has evaporated and the ingredients are cooked enough, the oil will split. The spice paste is now ready to receive the remaining ingredients.

Some important tips:

- Cook over medium heat. Constantly monitor the temperature to prevent the paste from burning and turning bitter.

- How long should it take? I'd say five to seven minutes. This is the minimum amount of time for the paste to reach its most flavorful and aromatic, and for the shallots and garlic to be mateng, or cooked. Sambals take twelve to fifteen minutes, sometimes longer depending on the amount.

- When making spice pastes in bulk, the longer you cook, the longer they will last. When cooked for at least thirty minutes, a spice paste can keep for up to six months sealed in a glass container and refrigerated.

Resources

Asian market chains with branches all over North America:

99 Ranch Market	99ranch.com
H-Mart	hmart.com
Seafood City	seafood city.com

Indonesian markets around the country, many will ship:

California

Holland International Market
9835 Belmont St, Bellflower, CA 90706
562-925-9444

Indo Culinair En Markt
43102 Christy St, Fremont, CA 94538
(408) 204-9166

ABC Indomart
345 N. State College Blvd, Fullerton, CA 92831
(714) 927-9400

Seattle

Maya Asian Market
19725 40th Ave W Ste A, Lynnwood, WA 98036
(425) 835-0593

Texas

Little Dutch Girl
210 Gentry St, Spring, TX 77373
(281) 355-0199

Midwest

Vander Veen's The Dutch Store
2755 28th St SW, Wyoming, MI 49519
(800) 813-9538

Waroeng – A Specialty Indonesian Market
2301 W. Schaumburg Rd, Schaumburg, IL 60194
(833) 927-6364

New England

Aneka Market
159 Rochester Hill Rd, Rochester, NH 03867
(603) 866-4923

NYC

Indo Java Groceries
85-12 Queens Blvd. #1 Queens, NY 11373
(718) 779-2241

OK Indo
8815 Justice Ave New York, NY 11373
(718) 606-0104

Philadelphia

Ramayana Store
1941 S. 8th St Philadelphia PA 19148
(267) 773-8882

Pendawa Enterprises Inc
1529 Morris St, Philadelphia, PA 19145
(215) 755-6229

Washington D.C. Metro

Ibu Campbell Indonesian and Asian Market
17162 Redland Rd, Derwood, MD 20855
(240) 654-3466

Online

Aneka Market	anekamarket.com
Indo Merchant	indomerchant.com
Indo Food Store	indofoodstore.com
Indo Groceries	indogroceries.com

Traditional Tempeh

BOSTempeh	bostempeh.com
WiwasTempeh	wiwastempeh.com

Acknowledgments

I first wrote my proposal for *Mortar and Pestle* in 2008. Yes, it was that long ago. After multiple submissions and countless rejections, I pretty much gave up hope that my book would ever be published traditionally. However, in 2021, my agent sent me an email message that started with: "You know I often equate this whole process to something like dating. Once you give up, then true love happens!" And the rest as they say, is history. (P/s Thank you, Clare Pelino for never giving up on me!)

This book has truly been a labor of love (and patience!). I couldn't have done it without the following people who were crucial to my book journey.

My mum, Julia, for teaching me how to cook the food of my homeland and constantly trying to keep us connected to our roots.

My dad, Rudy, for teaching me that "You can't argue with taste."

My siblings, Mars and Maureen, for well, being my siblings, the only other relations who experienced growing up in the Singapore clan of the Tanumihardja family.

My husband, Omar, and son, Isaac, for eating everything I cook, whether tasty or not!

The editorial and design team at Weldon Owen: editor Amy Marr, art director Chrissy Kwasnik, book designer Debbie Berne, and associate art director Meg Bingham.

The photography team at Waterbury Publications: photographer Ken Carlson, food stylist Joshua Hake, and food styling assistant T. Myers.

Thank you to family and friends—old and new—in Indonesia.

Cousins Gratia Ali Noverita and Arry Tantra, Hanny "Ping-Ping" Lay, and tante Yeni Ligawati for shuttling me around on food excursions.

Tante Yenny Andiani and cousins Sherley Winata and Antony Pranata for their kind hospitality.

Om William Wongso for being a constant source of inspiration and support.

Professor Murdijati Gardjito, Astrid Enricka Dhita and Santhi Serad for expanding my knowledge of regional Indonesian cuisine.

Dewi Novita Sari for opening up her home kitchen and cooking her special plant-based recipes with me.

My guides Sutarya Nyoman Mangkok and Putu Nopriawan "Gabong" for showing me around Bali.

Chef Theodora Poerdisastra for a friendship forged over tempeh-making.

Chef Yudiawan for teaching me the intricacies of Balinese cuisine.

And, I'm so grateful for my recipe testers, some of whom have been with me for several cookbooks (you know who you are!).

Marcie Flinchum Atkins
Dave Brewer and Jane Hodges
Jeanne Bulla
Naomi Capili
Ivy Chan
Suzana Dharma
Paula Enguidanos
Emily Hilderman
Luwei Hioe
David Jacobs and Sylvia Liu
Emily Leung
Sharon Lim
Laura McCarthy
Nicole Oandasan
Lani Randle
Madelyn Rosenberg
Debra Samuels
Traca Savadogo
Niki Stojnic
Liese Timmermann
Samantha Wetzler

About the Authors

Patricia Tanumihardja was born in Jakarta, Indonesia, grew up in Singapore, and moved to the United States at the age of nineteen. Her culinary training began as a little girl at her mother's side in their always busy home kitchen. Today, she is a food writer who has appeared in such print and online publications as *Saveur*, *edible Seattle*, Epicurious.com. and SeriousEats.com. She is the author of four cookbooks and lives in Virginia with her husband and son.

Juliana Evari Suparman was born in Bekasi, Indonesia, and lived in Singapore for thirty years, where she was a floral designer and an avid home cook who prepared food for house parties, church events, and her family. In 2002, Juliana and her husband, Rudy Tanumihardja, moved to Seattle to be with their children and grandsons. There, she became an active member of the local Indonesian community and parlayed her experience into a restaurant and catering business, a natural extension of her passion for community, family, and food.

Index

weldon**owen**

an imprint of Insight Editions
P.O. Box 3088
San Rafael, CA 94912
www.weldonowen.com

CEO Raoul Goff
Publisher Roger Shaw
Publishing Director Katie Killebrew
Associate Publisher Amy Marr
VP Creative Chrissy Kwasnik
Associate Art Director Megan Sinead Bingham
Production Designer Jean Hwang
VP Manufacturing Alix Nicholaeff
Sr Production Manager Joshua Smith
Sr Production Manager, Subsidiary Rights Lina s Palma-Temena

Designer Debbie Berne

Food Photography by Waterbury Publications Inc.

Weldon Owen would also like to thank the following people for their work and support in producing this book: Kris Balloun, Jessica Easto, and Elizabeth Parson.

Text © 2024 Patricia Tanumihardja and Juliana Evari Suparman

ISBN: 978-1-68188-926-9

Manufactured in China by Insight Editions

10 9 8 7 6 5 4 3 2 1

The information in this book is provided as a resource for inspiration and education. Author and Publisher expressly disclaim any responsibility for any adverse effects from the use or application of the information contained in this book. Neither the Publisher nor Author shall be liable for any losses suffered by any reader of this book.

 ROOTS of PEACE ⊕ REPLANTED PAPER

Insight Editions, in association with Roots of Peace, will plant two trees for each tree used in the manufacturing of this book. Roots of Peace is an internationally renowned humanitarian organization dedicated to eradicating land mines worldwide and converting war-torn lands into productive farms and wildlife habitats. Roots of Peace will plant two million fruit and nut trees in Afghanistan and provide farmers there with the skills and support necessary for sustainable land use.